GW00994223

The
WISDOM
of
THE KABBALAH

OTHER TITLES IN THIS SERIES

The Wisdom of the Ancient Greeks, ISBN 1–85168–298–8

The Wisdom of the Arabs, ISBN 1–85168–283–X

The Wisdom of the Bahá'í Faith, ISBN 1–85168–282–1

The Wisdom of Buddhism, ISBN 1–85168–226–0

The Wisdom of the Confucians, ISBN 1–85168–259–7

The Wisdom of Hinduism, ISBN 1–85168–227–9

The Wisdom of Jesus, ISBN 1–85168–225–2

The Wisdom of Judaism, ISBN 1–85168–228–7

The Wisdom of the Qur'an, ISBN 1–85168–224–4

The Wisdom of Sikhism, ISBN 1–85168–280–5

The Wisdom of Sufism, ISBN 1–85168–260–0

The Wisdom of the Tao, ISBN 1–85168–232–5

The Wisdom of Zen, ISBN 1–85168–281–3

The
WISDOM
of
THE KABBALAH

Compiled by Dan Cohn-Sherbok

ONEWORLD

OXFORD

THE WISDOM OF THE KABBALAH

Oneworld Publications
(Sales and Editorial)
185 Banbury Road
Oxford OX2 7AR
England
www.oneworld-publications.com

ISBN 1–85168–297–X

Cover and text design by Design Deluxe, Bath
Typeset by Cyclops Media Productions
Printed and bound by Graphicom Srl, Vicenza, Italy

CONTENTS

Introduction   vii
List of pictures   xxii

GOD   23
  Infinite   24
  Creation   28
  Emanation   38
  Incomprehensibility   49
  Mystery   53
  Divine Presence   56
  Providence   62
  Angels   63

THE MYSTIC WAY   65
  Chariot   66
  Heavenly Ascent   76
  God's Names   82
  Alphabet   89
  Unity   91
  Asceticism   99
  Cleaving to God   106
  Cosmic Repair   111
  Soul   114
  Study   121

Perfection 126

Prayer 129

Spiritual Master 134

Meditation 139

Fear of God 147

Love of God 150

Glory 153

Prophecy 160

Martyrdom 163

HUMAN BEINGS 165

Good 166

Evil 173

Commandments 178

Humility 185

Charity 189

Joy 190

Hypocrisy 192

Sin 194

Poverty 198

Torah 199

Wisdom 201

Glossary 204

Chronological Table 205

Acknowledgements 208

INTRODUCTION

Jewish mysticism

In the world's faiths the central aim of mysticism is to attain an apprehension of a union with the Divine. Within Judaism, the mystic is understood as one who seeks to gain an experience of God – this can be attained either through personal experience or intense speculation. In the history of the faith, mysticism has undergone a complex evolution, beginning with the experiences of the patriarchs to the cosmological and theological explanations of later rabbis contained in *Kabbalah* (Jewish mysticism). Yet, despite their differences in approach, Jewish thinkers have been united in their conviction that the spiritual quest is of paramount importance. The purpose of the religous life, they maintain, is to know God and experience his divine presence.

The Hebrew experiences contain some of the most vivid and arresting depictions of divine encounter. According to tradition, prophecy culminated during the period of the Second Temple (sixth century BCE–first century CE). In the place of charismatic figures claiming to have had a direct

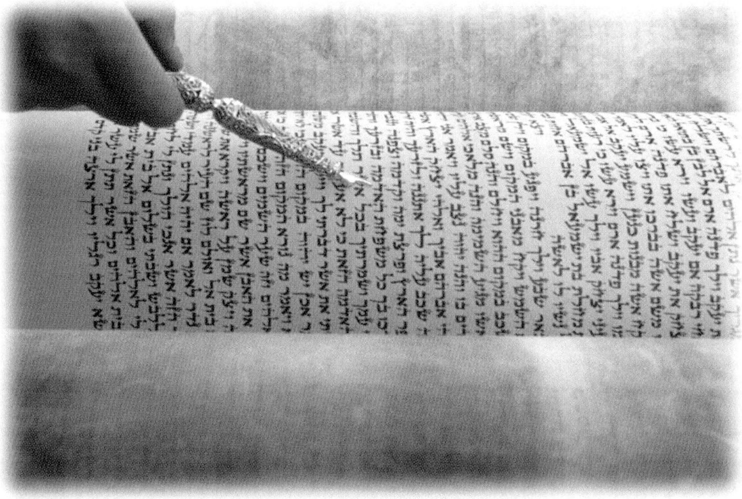

experience of God, Jewish writers engaged in speculation about the nature of God and his relation to the world. Initially such theorizing was contained in biblical books as well as in non-canonical literature. Later, Hellenistic thinkers, such as the first-century philosopher Philo of Alexandria, formulated theories regarding God's mediation in the cosmos. Drawing on Neoplatonic ideas, these writers argued that God has contact with the world through divine agencies.

Within early rabbinic literature, Jewish sages also engaged in theological speculation based on the biblical text. These doctrines were frequently of a secret nature. In this regard, the first chapter of the book of Ezekiel played an important role in early rabbinic mysticism. In this biblical text the *Merkavah* (divine chariot) is described in detail, and this scriptural source served as the basis for rabbinic speculation about the nature of the Deity. It was the aim of the mystic to be a '*Merkavah* rider' so that he would be able to penetrate the heavenly mysteries. Within this contemplative system, the rabbis believed that the pious could free themselves from the fetters of bodily existence and enter paradise.

A further dimension of this theory was that certain pious individuals could temporarily ascend into the unseen realm and, having learnt the deepest secrets, return to earth. These mystics were able to attain a state of ecstasy, to behold visions and hear voices. As students of the *Merkavah* they were the ones able to attain the highest degree of spiritual insight. A description of the experiences of these *Merkavah* mystics is contained in *Hekhalot* (heavenly hall) literature from the seventh to the eleventh century CE. In order to make their heavenly ascent, these mystics followed strict ascetic disciplines, including fasting, ablution and the invocation of God's name. After reaching a state of ecstasy, the mystic was able to enter the seven heavenly halls and attain a vision of the divine chariot.

Closely associated with this form of speculation were mystical theories about creation. Within rabbinic sources the rabbis discussed the hidden meaning of the Genesis narrative. The most important early treatise, possibly from the second century CE, that describes the process of creation, is the *Sefer Yetsirah* (Book of Creation). According to this cosmological text, God created the universe by thirty-two mysterious paths, consisting of twenty-two letters of the Hebrew alphabet together with ten *sefirot* (divine emanations).

This mysterious doctrine was supplemented by a theory of divine emanation through the ten *sefirot*. The first of the *sefirot* is the spirit of the living God; air is the second and is derived from the first – on it are hewn the twenty-two letters. The third of the *sefirot* is the water that comes from the air.

The fourth is the fire that comes from water, through which God made the heavenly wheels, the seraphim and the ministering angels. The remaining six *sefirot* are the six dimensions of space – north, south, east, west, height and depth.

These mystical texts of early rabbinic Judaism were studied by Jewish settlers in the Rhineland from approximately the ninth century. During the twelfth and thirteenth centuries these authorities – the *Hasidei Ashkenaz* (pious men of Germany) – delved into *Hekhalot* (heavenly hall) literature and the *Sefer Yetsirah*, as well as philosophical works. In their writings these mystics were preoccupied with the mystery of divine unity. The aim of German mysticism was to attain a vision of God's glory through the cultivation of the life of *hasiduth* (pietism), which embraced devotion, saintliness and contemplation.

Parallel with this development in Germany, Jewish mystics in southern France were engaged in mystical speculation about the nature of God, the soul, the existence of evil and the religious life. In twelfth-century Provence the *Bahir* (The Book of Light) reinterpreted the concept of the *sefirot* as depicted in the *Sefer Yetsirah*. According to the Bahir, the sefirot were conceived of as vessels, crowns or words that constitute the structure of the divine realm. Basing themselves on this

anonymous work, various Jewish sages of Provence engaged in similar mystical reflection. Thus Isaac the Blind conceived of the sefirot as emanations from a hidden dimension of the Godhead.

In Gerona the traditions from Isaac the Blind were broadly disseminated. One of the most important of these Geronese kabbalists was Azriel of Gerona, who replaced divine thought with divine will as the first emanation of the *Ayn Sof* (Infinite). The most famous figure of this circle was Moses ben Nahman, known as Nahmanides, who helped this mystical school gain general acceptance. During the time that these Geronese mystics were propounding their kabbalistic theories, different mystical schools developed in other parts of Spain. Influenced by the *Hasidei Ashkenaz* and the Sufi traditions of Isalm, Abraham Abulafia wrote meditative texts on the technique of combining the letters of the alphabet as a means of realizing human aspirations towards prophecy.

Another Spanish kabbalist, Isaac ibn Latif, also attempted to elaborate ideas found in Moses Maimonides' *Guide for the Perplexed*. For ibn Latif, the primeval will was the source of all emanation. Adopting Neoplatonic conceptions, he argued that from the first created thing emanated all the other stages, referred to symbolically as light, fire, ether and water. According to ibn Latif, *kabbalah* is superior to philosophy.

Other Spanish kabbalists were more attracted to gnostic ideas. Isaac ha-Kohen, for example, elaborated the theory of a demonic emanation whose ten spheres were counterparts of the holy *sefirot*. The mingling of such gnostic teaching with the *kabbalah* of Gerona resulted in the publication of the major mystical work of Spanish Jewry, the *Zohar* (The Book of Splendour), composed by the thirteenth-century writer Moses ben Shem Tov de Leon in Guadalajara – although the author placed the work in the setting of the second century CE, focusing on Rabbi Simeon bar Yochai.

According to these various kabbalistic systems, God in himself lies beyond any speculative comprehension. To express the unknowable aspect of the Divine, early kabbalists of Provence and Spain referred to the divine Infinite as *Ayn Sof*. The *Ayn Sof* does not reveal itself; it is beyond all thought and at times is identified with the Aristotelian First Cause. In kabbalistic teaching, creation is bound up with the manifestation of the hidden God and his outward movement. According to the *Zohar*, the *sefirot* emanate from the hidden depths of the Godhead like a flame.

For the kabbalists the existence of evil was a central issue. According to one tradition evil has no objective reality. Another view, as propounded in the *Bahir*, depicts the *sefirah* of power as an attribute whose name is evil. On the basis of such a teaching Isaac the Blind concluded that there must be a positive root of evil and death. In the *Zohar*, there is a detailed hierarchical structure of this emanation, in which the *Sitra Ahra* (the other side) is depicted as having ten *sefirot* of its own. The evil in the universe, the *Zohar* explains, has its origins in the leftovers of worlds that were destroyed. According to the *Zohar*, evil is like the bark of a tree of emanation; it is a husk or shell in which lower dimensions of existing things are encased.

For mystics the doctrine of a hidden God who brings about creation had important implications for the kabbalistic view of humankind. The biblical idea that human beings were created in the image of God implies that they are modelled on the *sefirot*, and are microcosms reflecting the nature of the cosmos. As far as souls are concerned, they are stored in one of the palaces in the sphere of *Beriyah* (Creation) where they are taught divine secrets. But when they enter the world of *Asiyah* (making), such knowledge disappears. According to some kabbalists, the body that houses the soul is the work of the *Sitra Ahra*; others contend that corporeality is neither intrinsically good nor bad. On the other hand, there were those who saw bodily processes as reflecting heavenly processes. In such a context the sexual union was regarded as metaphysically significant.

The mystic deeds of *tikkun* (repair) sustain the world, activate nature to praise God, and bring about the coupling of the tenth and the sixth *sefirot*. Such repair is accomplished by keeping the commandments, which are conceived of as vessels for establishing contact with the Godhead and for ensuring divine mercy. Such a religious life provided the kabbalist with a means of integrating into the divine hierarchy of creation – the *kabbalah* was able to guide the soul back to its source in the Infinite. The supreme rank attainable by the soul at the end of its sojourn is *devekut*, the mystical cleaving to God.

In ascending the higher worlds, the path of prayer parallels the observance of God's commandments. Yet unlike the commandments, prayer is independent of action and can become a process of meditation. Mystical prayer accompanied by meditative intentions, focusing on each prayer's kabbalistic content, is a feature of the various systems of *kabbalah*. For the kabbalists, prayer was seen as the ascent of the individual into the higher realms, where the soul could integrate with the higher spheres.

By using the traditional liturgy in a symbolic fashion, prayer repeats the hidden processes of the cosmos. At the time of prayer, the hierarchy of the upper realms is revealed as one of the names of God. Such disclosure is what constitutes the mystical activity of the individual in prayer, as

the kabbalist concentrates on the name that belongs to the domain through which his prayer is passing. The intention involved in mystic prayer is seen as a necessary element in the mystery of heavenly unification that brought the Divine down to the lowest realm and tied the *sefirot* to each other and the *Ayn Sof*.

In addition to mystical meditation, the kabbalists make use of the letters of the alphabet and of the names of God for the purposes of meditative training. By engaging in the combination of letters and names, the mystic is able to empty his mind so as to concentrate on divine matters. Through such experiences the kabbalists believed they could attempt to conduct the soul to a state of the highest rapture in which divine reality was disclosed.

In the early modern period Safed in Israel had become a major centre of Jewish religious life. In this town mystics also participated in various ascetic practices such as fasting, public confessions of sins, wearing sackcloth and ashes, and praying at the graves of venerable sages. In this centre of kabbalistic activity one of the greatest mystics of Safed, Moses Cordovero, collected, organized and interpreted the teachings of earlier mystic authors. Later in the sixteenth century kabbalistic speculation was transformed by the greatest mystic of Safed, Isaac Luria. By the beginning of the seventeenth century

Lurianic mysticism had made a major impact on Sephardic Jewry, and messianic expectations had also become a central feature of Jewish life. In this milieu the arrival of a self-proclaimed messianic king, Shabbetai Zevi, brought about a transformation of Jewish life and thought.

By the middle of the eighteenth century the Jewish community had suffered numerous waves of persecution and was deeply dispirited by the conversion of Shabbetai Zevi. In this enviroment the Hasidic movement – grounded in *kabbalah* – sought to revitalize Jewish life. In the medieval period the *Hasidei Ashkenaz* attempted to achieve perfection through various mystical activities. This tradition was carried on by Lurianic kabbalists who engaged in various forms of self-mortification. In opposition to such ascetic practices, the Baal Shem Tov, the founder of Hasidism, and his followers emphasized the omnipresence of God rather than the shattering of the vessels and the imprisonment of divine sparks by the powers of evil. For Hasidic Judaism there is no place where God is absent. The doctrine of divine contraction was interpreted by Hasidic sages as only an apparent withdrawal of the divine presence. Divine light, they believed, is everywhere.

For some Hasidim, *devekut* (cleaving to God) in prayer was understood as the annihilation of selfhood and the ascent of the soul to the divine light. In this context, joy, humility, gratitude and spontaneity are seen as essential features of Hasidic worship. The central obstacles to concentration in prayer are distracting thoughts. For the Hasidim, it is possible to achieve *devekut* in daily activities including drinking, business affairs and sex. Such ordinary acts become religious if in performing them one cleaves to God, and *devekut* is thus attainable by all Jews. Unlike the earlier mystical tradition, Hasidism provided a means by which ordinary Jews could reach a state of spiritual ecstasy.

Another central feature of this new movement was the institution of the *zaddik* (holy person) or *rebbe* (spiritual leader), which gave expression to a widespread disillusionment with rabbinic leadership. According to Hasidism, the *zaddikim* were spiritually superior individuals who had attained the highest level of *devekut*. The goal of the *zaddik* was to elevate the souls of his flock to the divine light. As an authoritarian figure, the *zaddik* was seen by his followers as possessing miraculous powers to ascend to the divine realm. From its inception at the end of the eighteenth century to the present day, this movement has kept alive the mystical traditions of the Jewish past.

PICTURES

Wheel of letters, from Pardes Rimmonim by   41
    Moses Cordovero, 1592

Model depicting the Divine word of the Sefirot, from Pardes   47
    Rimmonim (see above)

Cherubim hovering over the ark of the tabernacle,   55
    from thirteenth century French manuscript

The Tree of Life   61

The four letter Name of God (Tetragrammaton), from fourteenth 68
    century Bible in Sefardi hand

The Face of the Long One, detail of Lurianic scheme from the   72
    nineteenth century

Amulet, from Shaar ha-Yihud by Hayyim Vital, sixteenth century 77

Detail from nineteenth century Lurianic scroll   72

Circles of instruction used in meditation, from maunscript of 85
    writings by Abraham Abulafia

Kabbalistic diagram, from the Book of Formation, Sefer Yezirah, 90
    Babylonia, sixth century

Hands inscribed with Kabbalistic symbols, from Shefa Tal, by   95
    Shabbetai Horowitz, 1712

Amulet to protect a mother during childbirth, from   110
    Book of Raziel, 1701

Rabbi Akiba, woodcut from Haggadah, sixteenth century   127

GOD

INFINITE

I F ONE should ask, 'Why should I believe in *Ayn Sof*?' you should tell him: You ought to know that everything which is visible or perceptible to the heart is finite. Every limited thing has an end and every finite thing is not perfect. Therefore, there must be that which is without limit and which is called *Ayn Sof*. It is absolute perfection in complete unity which does not change. If it is without limit, there is nothing beside it. Since it is sublime, it is the root of all things visible and unseen. Since it is hidden, it is the basis of faith and of disbelief. The masters of speculation admit that we are unable to grasp it except by saying what it is not.

AZRIEL OF GERONA

T HE DENIAL of corporeality means that God is not limited and is neither a body nor a force in a body. The principle of this negation is that God is not limited by either place or time. For He is, was and always will be.

Sefer Maarekhet ha-Elohut

A T THE very beginning the king made engravings in the supernal purity. A spark of blackness emerged in the sealed within the sealed, from the mystery of *Ayn Sof*, a mist within matter, implanted in a ring, no white, no black, no red, no yellow, no colour at all.

Zohar

R ABBI ELEAZAR asked Rabbi Simeon: 'We know that the whole-offering is connected to the Holy of Holies so that it may be illumined. To what heights does the attachment of the will of the priests, the Levites and Israel extend?' He said, 'We have already taught that it extends to *Ayn Sof* [Infinite] since all attachment, unification and completion is to be secreted in that secret which is not perceived or known, and which contains the will of all wills. *Ayn Sof* cannot be known, it does not produce end or beginning like the primal *ayin* [nothing], which does bring forth beginning and end … there are no end, no wills, no lights, no luminaries in *Ayn Sof*.

Zohar

WOE TO one who compares *Ayn Sof*
to any of the human characteristics
or even to one of His own attributes,
all the more so to one who compares Him to humans
    …
who are born and die.
Ayn Sof may be characterized according to His
   governance
upon a particular attribute
or even upon all the created beings.
When He disappears
above and beyond that attribute,
He cannot be said to have that attribute,
characteristic or form.

Zohar

CREATION

I N THE beginning God created. 'In the beginning' – a primeval mystery; 'created' – a concealed mystery from which all extends; 'God' – a mystery that supports all below.

Zohar

' A ND GOD said: Let there be light. And there was light' (Gen. 1:3). From here we can begin to find hidden mysteries, how the world was created in detail.

Zohar

L ET YOUR ears hear what your mouth speaks. Have I not just told you that there is that which is called 'the cause of causes', and this is not the same as that which is called 'cause above all causes', for 'cause above all causes' has no companion from which it can take advice, for it is single, preceding all, with no partner, and it is for this reason that it says, 'See now that I, even I, am He, and there is no god with me.'

Zohar

ELIJAH BEGAN and said: 'Master of the worlds. You are one but not in number; you are the highest of the high, the secret of all secrets; you are altogether beyond the reach of thought. You are He that produced ten *tikkunim* [restorations], which we call ten *sefirot* [divine emanations], so that through them you might guide the secret worlds that are not revealed, and the worlds that are revealed. And through them you are concealed from mankind and you bind them and unite them. Since you are within, whoever separates one of the ten from its fellow is thought of as making a separation in you.

Zohar

MASTER OF the worlds,
You are the cause of causes,
the first cause
who waters the Tree from your spring.
This spring is like the soul to the body,
the life of the body.
Nothing can be compared to you,
within or without.

You created the heavens and the earth,
the sun and the moon,
the stars and constellations.

Tikkunei Zohar

THREE MOTHERS: *aleph*, *mem*, *shin*. A great secret, wonderful and hidden. He seals them with six rings. From them go out: air, fire and water. From them the fathers are born. From the fathers, the progeny.

Three mothers: *aleph*, *mem*, *shin*. He engraved them. He hewed them. He combined them. He weighed them. He set them at opposites. He formed through them: three mothers – *aleph*, *mem*, *shin* in the universe; three mothers – *aleph*, *mem* and *shin* in the year; three mothers – *aleph*, *mem* and *shin* in the body of male and female.

Three mothers: *aleph*, *mem*, *shin*. The product of fire is heaven; the product of air is air; the product of water is earth. Fire is above; water is below; air tips the balance between them. From them, the fathers were generated, and from them, everything is created.

Sefer Yetsirah

H E CAUSED the letter *bet* to reign over life ... He formed through them: Saturn in the universe, the first day in the year, and the right eye in the body of male and female.

He caused the letter *gimel* to reign over peace ... He formed through them: Jupiter in the universe, the second day in the year, and the left eye in the body of male and female.

He caused the letter *dalet* to reign over wisdom ... He formed through them: Mars in the universe, the third day in the year, and the right ear in the body of male and female.

He caused the letter *kaf* to reign over wealth ... He formed through them: Sun in the universe, the fourth day in the year, and the left ear of the body of male and female.

He caused the letter *pey* to reign over gracefulness ... He formed through them: Venus in the universe, the fifth day in the year, and the right nostril of the body of male and female.

He caused the letter *resh* to reign over seed ... He formed through them: Mercury in the universe, the sixth day in the year, and the left nostril in the body of male and female.

He caused the letter *tav* to reign over dominion ... He formed through them: Moon in the universe, the Sabbath day in the year, and the mouth in the body of male and female.

Sefer Yetsirah

TWELVE SIMPLE letters: *hey, vav, zayin, chet, tet, yod, lamed, nun, samech, ayin, tsade, kof.* He engraved their foundations, He hewed them out, He combined them, He weighed them, and He set them at opposites, and He formed through them: twelve constellations in the universe, twelve months in the year, twelve organs in the body of male and female.

Sefer Yetsirah

A CERTAIN KING dwelt within the inner chamber of his palace. There were thirty-two chambers in all and each chamber had its own path.

Now is it proper for everyone to come to the king's chamber by simply following all the paths? Of course not.

And is it proper for the king to openly reveal his pearls, brocades and hidden, precious treasures? Of course not.

So what did the king do? He appointed his daughter and set in her and in her garments all the different pathways. Another who wishes to enter the palace should not look at her.

Pesikta de-Rav Kahana

ALL CREATURES were created because of the good inherent in them.

JUDAH LOEW OF PRAGUE

HE SHOULD cultivate the quality of fervour. He should rise from sleep with fervour for he has been renewed and has become a new person, and is capable of creating, and resembles the Holy One, praised be He, who created worlds.

BAAL SHEM TOV

BEFORE THE Holy One, blessed be He, created this world, He went on creating worlds and destroying them. Whatsoever exists in this world, everything that has been in existence throughout all generations, was in existence in His presence in all their manifold forms.

Zohar

HE MADE this world of below to correspond with the world of above. Everything which is above has its pattern here below and all constitutes a unity.

Zohar

BEFORE HAVING created any shape in the world, before having produced any form, He was alone, without form, resembling nothing. Who could comprehend Him as He then was, before creation, since He had no form? It is forbidden to picture Him by any form or under any shape whatsoever.

Zohar

THERE IS nothing which is not in Him. He has a shape, and one can say that He has no shape. In assuming a shape, He has given existence to all things.

Zohar

THE GOAL of creating man is that he might become submissive to God. This is to be explained as follows: the descent of the divine potency through many stages of self-limitation was to serve as a prelude to its return upwards in order to transform darkness into light. It is for this role that God created man on earth.

SHNEUR ZALMAN OF LIADY

misrt:

Cead

fui qu

uic·m

consul

uiuer

Ang

the so

occur

& dic

misrt

EMANATION

ONE: SPIRIT of living *Elohim*, blessed and blest is the name of Him who lives forever ... His beginning has no beginning; His end has no end.

Two: spiritual air from spirit. He engraved and hewed out in it twenty-two letters as a foundation: three mothers, seven doubles, and twelve simples. They are of one spirit.

Three: spiritual water from spiritual air. He engraved and hewed out in it chaos and disorder, mud and mire. He engraved it like a type of furrow. He raised it like a type of wall. He surrounded it like a type of ceiling. He poured snow over them and it became earth, as it is said, 'For He said to the snow, be earth' (Job 37:6).

Four: spiritual fire from spiritual water. He engraved and hewed out in it the Throne of Glory, seraphim and ophanim and *hayyot*, and ministering angels. From the three of them He established His dwelling place, as it is said, 'Who makes winds His messengers, the flaming fire His ministers' (Psalms 104:4).

He chose three of the simple letters, sealed them with spirit and set them into his great name, YHV, and sealed through them six extremities. Five: He sealed height; He turned upwards and sealed it with YHV. Six: He sealed abyss; He turned downwards, and sealed it with YHV. Seven: He sealed east; He turned forwards and sealed it with HYV. Eight; He sealed west; He turned backwards and sealed it with HYV. Nine: He sealed south; He turned right and sealed it with VYH. Ten: He sealed north; He turned left and sealed it with VHY.

These ten intangible *sefirot* are One – spirit of living *Elohim*; spiritual air from spirit; spiritual water from spiritual air; spiritual fire from spiritual water; height, abyss, east, west, north and south.

Sefer Yetsirah

RABBI SHIMON said:
I raise my hands upward in prayer.
When the divine will up above
shines upon the will
which is eternally unknown and imperceptible,
the first hidden upper will
produces its unknown creation
and radiates what it does secretly.
Then, the will of divine thought
pursues the first will
in order to be illuminated by it.
A curtain is then opened

and, from inside, with the divine will
pursuing the upper will,
it reaches and yet does not reach up
and the curtain begins to radiate.
Then, the divine thought
is illuminated secretly
and remains unknown, hidden.
The illumination coming from
the hidden upper unknown will strike the
light of the curtain
which is lit up by the will
which is unknown, unknowable and concealed.

Zohar

ZOHAR, CONCEALED of the concealed, struck its aura.
The aura touched and did not touch this point.
Then this beginning emanated
and made itself a palace for its glory and its praise.
There it sowed the seed of holiness
to give birth
for the benefit of the universe.

Zohar

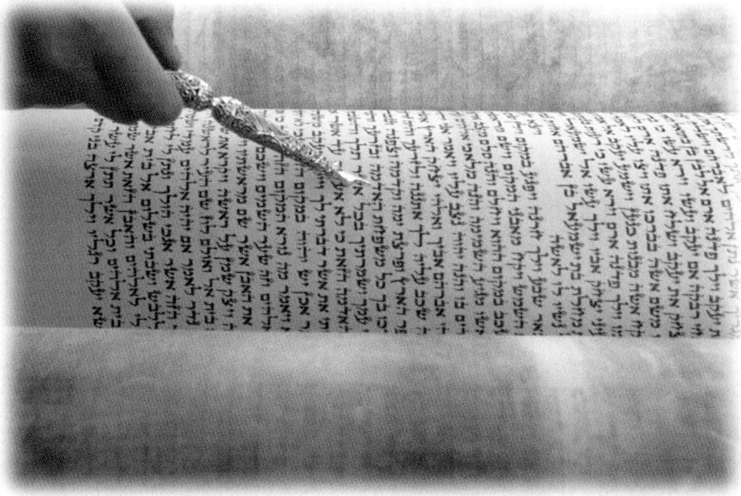

THE LORD, the Lord of hosts, the God of Israel, the living God and the King of the Universe, the Almighty, Merciful and Gracious, the Exalted, who abides in eternity, whose name is august and holy, shaped and created the universe with thirty-two wondrous paths of wisdom, comprising three categories: numbers, letters and words.

Ten non-corporeal *sefirot* (divine emanations) and twenty-two basic letters, three 'mother' letters, seven double letters, and twelve simple letters.

Ten non-corporeal *sefirot*, corresponding to the ten fingers, five paralleling five, with the covenant of unity in the centre, as indicated by the term for 'word' which is formed by tongue and mouth, and which also defines the organ that bears the covenant of circumcision.

Ten non-corporeal *sefirot*, ten and not nine, ten and not eleven; understand with wisdom, and discern with understanding; analyse them and probe them, clarify the matter and establish the Creator on His throne.

Ten non-corporeal *sefirot*. They comprise ten dimensions; the dimension of beginning, the dimension of end, the dimension of good, the dimension of evil, the dimension of height, the dimension of depth, the dimension of east, the dimension of west, the dimension of north, the dimension of south. One Lord alone, God, the faithful King, rules over all from His holy abode for ever and ever.

Ten non-corporeal *sefirot*. Their appearance is like a flash of lightning and they have no end. His word is in them, surging forth and receding. They hasten like a whirlwind to do his bidding and they bow down before His throne.

Ten non-corporeal *sefirot*. Their end is merged with their beginning and their beginning is merged with their end, as a flame is joined to the burning coal. For the Lord is one and there is none like him, and what can you count before One.

Ten non-corporeal *sefirot*. Curb your mouth from speaking of them and your heart from speculating about them. And if your mouth ventures to speak and your heart to speculate, turn back. For this reason it is written 'And the living creatures surged forward and returned' (Ezek. 1:14).

Sefer Yetsirah

WHY WAS Aaron's blessing pronounced with the raising of the hands? He could have blessed them by pronouncing the blessing. The reason is that there are ten fingers in the hands, an allusion to the ten *sefirot* [divine emanations] with which heaven and earth were finished.

Bahir

THEN, *AYN SOF* contracted Himself into a central point with his light in the middle. He contracted this light and then removed Himself to the sides encircling the point at the centre. This left an empty place, an ether, and a vacuum around the point at the centre. This contraction, equidistant all around the point at the centre, formed a void in such a way that the vacuum was spherical on all sides in equal measure. It did not form a cube with right angles because *Ayn Sof* contracted Himself into a sphere in equal distance on all sides. He intended that the light of *Ayn Sof* should be in absolute equanimity. This necessitated that He contract himself in equal measure on all sides no more on one side than any other.

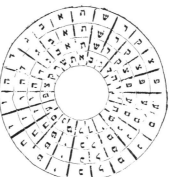

HAYYIM VITAL

AFTER THIS contraction, there was only the vacuum, ether and empty space in the midst of the light of *Ayn Sof*. There was now place for the emanations, creations, formations and actions.

HAYYIM VITAL

HOKHMAH [WISDOM] spread out and brought forth *Binah*
    [understanding].
They were found to be male and female.
Hokhmah, the father, and
Binah, the mother.
Then, these two united and
Lighted up each other.
The mother conceived and gave birth to a son.
Through the birth of a son,
The mother and father found perfection.
This led to the completion of everything,
the inclusion of everything –
father, mother, son and daughter.

Zohar

WHEN THE light becomes too strong, the receptacle disintegrates due to its limited capacity to contain the powerful light.

HAYYIM VITAL

FIRST OF all, the expansion burst through and produced a single hidden point from its own mystery.

Zohar

ONE WHO wishes to attain from God what he desires must contemplate the ten *sefirot*.

JOSEPH GIKATILLA

INCOMPREHENSIBILITY

I WILL tell of your glory
Though I have not seen you;
I will speak of you in similes
Though I cannot know your essence.

Hymn of Glory

HE UNDERSTANDS all, yet there is none that understands Him.

Zohar

ELIJAH SAID, 'Master of the world, you are one but not in number. You are the highest of the high, the secret of all secrets. You are altogether beyond the reach of thought.'

Zohar

YOU ARE wise but not with a known wisdom.

Zohar

MASTER OF the worlds,
You are one but not according to number.
You are elevated above all heights,
more hidden than all hidden things.
No thought apprehends you at all.
You are He who brought forth then perfections
which we call the ten *sefirot* [divine emanations]
through which you govern the worlds,
hidden, concealed and revealed.
Because there are ten *sefirot*,
You are also hidden from man.
You join the *sefirot* together
and cause them to be one.
Since you are present in them,
one who considers one in isolation from the rest
is considered himself
as one who thinks of you
as having separate parts.

Tikkunei Zohar

THERE IS no one who knows you at all,
and there is nothing as unique or unified as you,
above or below.
You are called the Lord of all.
You have no proper name since
You are the very essence of the divine names,
the perfection of the names.
When you are withdrawn from your names,
they are left
like a body without a soul.

Tikkunei Zohar

THERE IS none that knows anything of you and besides you there is no singleness and no unity in the upper and lower worlds, and you are acknowledged as Lord over all.

Zohar

THE ANCIENT One, the most hidden of the hidden, is a high beacon, and we know Him only by His lights, which illuminate our eyes so abundantly.

Zohar

THE MOST Ancient One is at the same time the most hidden of the hidden. He is separated from all things, and is at the same time not separated from all things. For all things are united in Him, and he unites Himself with all things.

Zohar

THAT WHICH a man comprehends in his mind of the divine, he cannot possibly communicate to others, to convey from the deep recesses of his own heart that which he has in heart and mind.

KALONYMUS KALMAN EPSTEIN

MYSTERY

HAPPY IS the portion of whoever can penetrate into the mysteries of his master and become absorbed into Him.

Zohar

IF YOU wish to enter into this mystery, concentrate on all that we have said. Contemplate the rooms that we have discussed, together with their lights, colours and letter combinations. Meditate on this for a while, either briefly or at length. Begin by placing your head between your knees.

JOSEPH TZAYACH

WHEN THE fingers are spread out on high a man honours God with numerous supernal mysteries. He demonstrates the mystery of the ten *sefirot* [divine emanations] as they are united and he blesses the Holy Name as it should be blessed.

ALEXANDER SUSSKIND

ZOHAR [BRIGHTNESS], sealed among the sealed things, made contact with its air, which touched, but did not touch, the point.

Zohar

'AND GOD said: Let the waters be gathered' (Gen. 1:9) – by means of a line, so that it should be by a straight path, for all emerged, while still hidden, from the mystery of the primal point until it reached and entered the supernal palace. From there it went forth in a straight line to the remaining levels, until it came to 'one place,' which brought all together in the totality of male and female.

Zohar

WHEN THE most secret of secrets sought to be revealed, He made, first of all, a single point, and this became thought. He made all the designs there; He did all the engravings there, and He engraved within the hidden holy luminary an engraving of a hidden design.

Zohar

WHATEVER THE Holy One, blessed be He, made, both above and below, is all in the mystery of male and female.

Zohar

DIVINE PRESENCE

HE IS to try and withdraw his mind from all else, and focus on the *Shekhinah* [Divine Presence].

BAAL SHEM TOV

AT THAT time the Holy One (blessed be He) wept, saying, 'Woe is me! What have I done! I caused my *Shekhinah* [Divine Presence] to dwell below for the sake of Israel, but now that Israel has sinned I have returned to my original dwelling place. Far be it from me that I should become a source of derision to the nations and a mockery to all creatures!' Immediately Metatron fell upon his face, exclaiming, 'O Sovereign of the universe, let me weep, but do not yourself weep!'

Lamentations Rabba

IN EVERY moment God is to be found.

DOV BAER OF MEZHIRICH

SWEET MELODIES will I sing to you
And hymns compose,
For my soul yearns for your presence
To know the mystery of your being.

Hymn of Glory

I T IS He that binds all the chariots of the angels, and binds them together; and He supports the upper and the lower worlds. And were He to remove himself from them they would have neither sustenance, knowledge or life.

Zohar

K NOW AND believe that there is a method involving the mystical purification of the limbs, through which it is possible for a human being to attach himself to the Divine Presence, even though it is a 'consuming fire'.

JOSEPH GIKATILLA

THOUGH GOD'S presence in the commandments is not visible to the naked eye, they link us with ties of love to the Creator.

MENAHEM MENDEL OF CHERNOBYL

THIS IS how one must condition himself to looking at things: if he suddenly found himself gazing at a beautiful woman, let him say to himself: How did she become this way? If she were dead she would not have this face, she would in fact be repellent. How then does she come to look this way? Obviously it comes to her because of a divine potency diffused in her which endows her face with colour and beauty. It thus turns out that the source of beauty is in the power of God.

BAAL SHEM TOV

WHEN ONE needs to discuss worldly matters he must realize that he is descending from the divine realm.

MENAHEM MENDEL OF VITEBSK

HE ENCOMPASSES all worlds, and none but He surrounds them on every side, above and below and in the four corners of the globe, and none may go beyond His domain. He fills all worlds, and no other fills them. He gives life to them, and there is no other god above Him to give Him life.

Zohar

HE BINDS and joins the species with one another, above and below, and there is no juncture of the four elements except by the Holy One, blessed be He, existing among them.

Zohar

THERE IS no place where He is not, above without end, and below without limit, and on every side there is no God but He.

Zohar

WOE TO the man who tries to hide himself from the Holy One, blessed be He, of whom it is written 'Do I not fill heaven and earth, says the Lord' (Jer. 23:24).

Zohar

IN ALL places, and especially in the synagogue where the *Shekhinah* [Divine Presence] is in front of you, sit in His presence in dread and set your heart to give thanks unto Him.

ELEAZAR BEN JUDAH OF WORMS

IN EVERY movement God is present since it is impossible to make any move or utter a word without the might of God.

DOV BAER OF MEZHIRICH

A PERSON MUST not pray for his own concerns; rather he is to pray that the *Shekhinah* [Divine Presence] be redeemed from exile.

DOV BAER OF MEZHIRICH

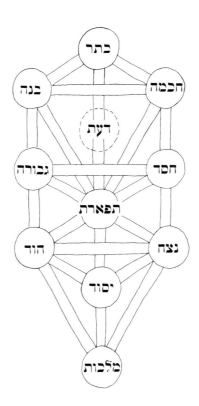

PROVIDENCE

WHATEVER HAPPENS, let him consider that it derives from God.

BAAL SHEM TOV

WE HAVE taught that this world is like a pattern of the world above, and, as for the world above, everything that happens in this world – so it is above.

Zohar

TO THE fish in the sea, whose eyes have no lids, whose eyes have no brows, for they do not sleep and do not need a protection for the eye. How much more is this true of the Most Ancient One. He needs no protection, especially since He supervises everything, nourishes everything, and does not sleep.

Zohar

ANGELS

OR GOD, not wishing to come down to the external senses, sends His own words [*logoi*] or angels in order to give assistance to those who love virtue. They attend like physicians to the diseases of the soul, apply themselves to heal them, offer sacred recommendations like sacred laws, and invite humans to practise the duties inculcated by them. Like the trainers and wrestlers, they implant in their pupils strength and power and irresistible vigour.

PHILO OF ALEXANDRIA

HE ANGEL Zagzagael, the prince of the inner court, told me: My friend, sit in my lap, and I will tell you what will happen to the Jewish people. I sat in his lap, and he looked at me and wept, and the tears dropped from his eyes and fell on my face.

Hekhalot Rabbati

THE WORLD above and the world below are perfectly balanced: Israel below, the angels above. Of the angels it is written: 'He makes his angels spirits' (Psalm 104:4). But when they descend, they put on the garment of this world. If they did not put on a garment befitting this world they could not endure in this world and the world could not endure them.

Zohar

BOTH GOOD and evil angels are created from a person's speech.

HAYYIM VITAL

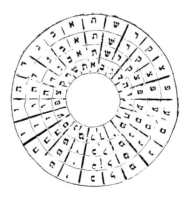

THE MYSTIC WAY

CHARIOT

IT IS said of Rabbi Johanan ben Zakkai that he was not ignorant of anything. He knew *Mishnah*, *Talmud*, law, exposition, grammatical analysis of the Torah, analysis of the scribes, logical inference, similar wordings, astronomical calculations, *gematriot* [mystical calculations], incantations for angels, incantations for demons, incantations to palm trees, proverbs of washerwomen, proverbs of foxes, a 'Great Thing' and a 'Small Thing'. A 'Great Thing' is the workings of the *Merkavah* [the Divine Chariot].

Talmud

ALL THOSE who go up to the *Merkavah* [Divine Chariot] are not harmed even though they see this entire set of palaces. And they descend in peace, returning and standing up to testify to the awesome, terrifying sight they have seen, the like of which cannot be seen in any of the palaces of flesh and blood.

Pirkei Hekhalot

WHAT IS it like to know the secret of the *Merkavah* [Divine Chariot]? It is like having a ladder in one's house and being able to go up and down at will.

Pirkei Hekhalot

SAID R. REHUMEI: What is the meaning of the verse (Prov. 6:23): 'The way of life is the reproof of instruction'? This teaches us that one who studies the work of creation and the work of the Chariot cannot but stumble, as it is written (Isa. 3:6): 'And this stumbling is under your hand.' These are matters that one cannot grasp unless one stumbles over them, and the Torah calls it 'the reproof of instruction', but in truth one thereby attains the path of life.

Bahir

WHOEVER TURNS his heart away from the affairs of the world and concerns himself with the work of the *Merkavah* [Divine Chariot], it is regarded by the Holy One, praised be He, as though he had prayed all day.

Bahir

מי לא יראך מלך הגוים כי לך יאתה כי בכל
חכמי הגוים ובכל מלכותם מאין כמוך :
יהוה

ELIEZER BEN Arach began his discourse on the mysteries of the *Merkavah* [Divine Chariot]. No sooner had he begun, than fire came down from heaven and encompassed all the trees of the field which, with one accord, burst into song.

Talmud

IT IS forbidden to explain the first chapters of Genesis to two persons, but it is only to be explained to one by himself. It is forbidden to explain the *Merkavah* [Divine Chariot] even to one by himself unless he be a sage and of an original turn of mind.

Mishnah

A CERTAIN youth was once explaining the *Hashmal* (Ezek. 1:27) when fire came forth and consumed him. When the question is asked, 'Why was this?' the answer is: 'His time had not yet come.'

Talmud

RABBI JOHANAN ben Zakkai was once riding on a donkey, and Rabbi Eliezer ben Arach was on a donkey behind him. The latter rabbi said to the former, 'O master! Teach me a chapter of the *Merkavah* [Divine Chariot] mysteries.' 'No!' replied the master. 'Have I not already informed you that the *Merkavah* may not be taught to any one man by himself unless he be a sage and of an original turn of mind?' 'Very well, then!' replied Eliezer ben Arach. 'Will you give me leave to tell you a thing which you have taught me?' 'Yes!' replied Johanan ben Zakkai. 'Say it!' The master dismounted from his donkey, wrapped himself up in a garment, and sat upon a stone beneath an olive tree. 'Why, O master, have you dismounted from your donkey?' asked the disciple. 'Is it possible,' he replied, 'that I will ride upon my donkey at the moment when you are expounding the mysteries of the *Merkavah*, and the *Shekhinah* [Divine Presence] is with us, and the ministering angels are accompanying us?' Rabbi Eliezer ben Arach opened his discourse on the mysteries of the *Merkavah*, and no sooner had he begun than fire came down from heaven and encompassed all the trees of the field, which, with one accord, burst into song.

Talmud

A FTER HE had created the form of the Heavenly Man, He used him as a *Merkavah* [Divine Chariot] on which to descend.

Zohar

P ERMISSION WAS granted to the proper, the meek, the humble, the wise, the upright, the pious, the chosen, the ascetics, the righteous, and the perfected ones to descend and ascend in the *Merkavah* [Divine Chariot].

Hekhalot Rabbati

O NE DARE not descend to the *Merkavah* [Divine Chariot] unless he has two qualifications. First, he must have read and reviewed the Torah, Prophets and Writings, and have mastered the *Mishnah*, the Law, the *Aggadah* [rabbinic scriptural commentary], as well as the deeper meaning of Law regarding what is permitted and what is forbidden. Second, he must be an individual who keeps the entire Torah, and heeds all of its prohibitions, decrees, judgements and laws, taught to Moses on Sinai.

Hekhalot Rabbati

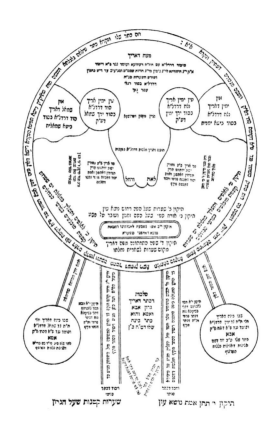

THE THRONGS of our companions stood, for they saw rivers of fire and brilliant flames separating them from us. Rabbi Nehunya ben Hakkanah sat and explained everything about the *Merkavah* [Divine Chariot]. He described its descent and ascent; how one who descends must descend, and how one who ascends must ascend.

Hekhalot Rabbati

THE GUARDS of the sixth palace make a practice of attacking those who descend and do not descend into the *Merkavah* [Divine Chariot] without authority. They throng around such individuals, striking them and burning them. They then send others in their places who do the same. They have no compunction, nor do they ever stop to ask, 'Why are we burning them? What enjoyment do we have when we assail those individuals who descend to the *Merkavah* and do not descend without authority?' This is the trait of the guardians at the door of the sixth chamber.

Hekhalot Rabbati

OUR RABBIS taught that four entered an orchard. These are they: Ben Azzai, Ben Zoma, Aher and Akiva. Akiva said to them, 'When you reach the stones of pure marble, do not say, "Water, water!" For it is said, "He who speaks falsehood shall not be established before my eyes."' Ben Azzai gazed and died. Concerning him Scripture says, 'Precious in the sight of the Lord is the death of his saints.' Ben Zoma gazed and was stricken. Concerning him Scripture says, 'Have you found honey? Eat as much as is sufficient for you, lest you be filled therewith, and vomit it.' Aher cut down the shoots. Akiva departed in peace.

Talmud

RABBI ISAAC said, 'It is a 500-year journey from the earth to the firmament, as it is said, "That your days may be multiplied, and the days of your chidren … as the days of the heaven upon the earth" (Deut. 11:21). The thickness of the firmament is a 500-year journey. The firmament contains only the sun, moon and stars but there is one *Merkavah* [Divine Chariot] therein.

The Vision of Ezekiel

As soon as the person entreats to descend to the *Merkavah* [Divine Chariot], Anpiel, the Prince, opens the doors of the seventh palace and that individual enters and stands on the threshold of the gate of the seventh palace. The holy *hayyot* [living creatures] lift him up. Five hundred and twelve eyes, and each and every eye of the eyes of the holy *hayyot* is hollow like the holes in a sieve woven of branches. These eyes appear like lightning, and they dart to and fro. In addition, there are the eyes of the cherubim of might and the wheels of the *Shekhinah* [Divine Presence], which are like torches of light and flames of burning coals. This person then trembles, shakes, moves to and fro, panics, is terrified, faints and collapses backwards.

Hekhalot Rabbatai

HEAVENLY ASCENT

YOU MAY perhaps know that many of the sages hold that when a man is worthy and blessed with certain qualities and he wishes to gaze at the heavenly chariot and the halls of the angels on high, he must follow certain exercises. He must fast for a specified number of days, he must place his head between his knees, whispering softly to himself the while certain praises of God with his face towards the ground. As a result he will gaze in the innermost recesses of his heart and it will seem as if he saw the seven halls with his own eyes, moving from hall to hall to observe that which is therein to be found.

HAI GAON

MAKE YOURSELF right. Meditate in a special place where your voice cannot be heard by others. Cleanse your heart and soul of all other thoughts in the world. Imagine that at this time your soul is separating itself from your body, and that you are leaving the physical world behind so that you enter the future world that is the source of all life.

ABRAHAM ABULAFIA

WHEN ONE is on a higher level, he can enter. He is brought in and led to the heavenly chambers where he is permitted to stand before the Throne of Glory. He then knows what will happen in the future, who will be raised up, who will be lowered, who will be made strong, who will be cut off, who will be made poor, who will be made rich, who will die, who will live, who will have his inheritance taken away from him, who will have it given to him, who will be invested with the Torah and who will be given wisdom.

Hekhalot Rabbati

WHEN ONE is on a higher level, all humanity stands before him like silver before a refiner who can distinguish which silver is pure and which is adulterated.

Hekhalot Rabbati

AN INDIVIDUAL thus ascends with the power of his concentration from one thing to the next, until he reaches the *Ayn Sof* [Infinite].

The Gate of Kavanah

I F ONE is pure and upright in deed, and if he grasps the cords of love existing in the holy roots of his soul, he will be able to ascend to every level in all the supernal universes.

MOSES CORDOVERO

T HE TRUE path is straight, depending on an individual's concentration. He must know how to concentrate on its truth with attachment of thought and desire derived from its unfathomable power. According to the strength of his concentration, he will then transmit power through his desire, desire through his knowledge, imagination through his thoughts, strength through his effort, and fortitude through his contemplation. When there is no other thought or desire intermingled with his concentration it can become so strong that it can transmit an influence from the *Ayn Sof* [Infinite] … An individual thus ascends with the strength of his concentration from one thing to the next, until he reaches the *Ayn Sof*.

AZRIEL OF GERONA

THE DISTANCE from the earth to the firmament is a journey of 500 years ... Above them are *hayyot* [the living creatures]. The feet of the holy are equal to all of them together. The ankles of the holy are equal to all of them. The legs of the holy are equal to all of them. The knees of the holy are equal to all of them. The thighs of the holy are equal to all of them. The bodies of the holy are equal to all of them. The necks of the holy are equal to all of them. The heads of the holy are equal to all of them. The horns of the holy are equal to all of them. Above them is the Throne of Glory. The feet of the Throne are equal to all of them. The Throne of Glory is equal to all of them. The King, the living and eternal God, high and exalted dwells above them.

Talmud

HE WHO goes down looks with a wondrous proudness and a strange powerfulness, with the proudness of exultation and the powerfulness of exultation and the powerfulness of radiance, for these two emotions are stirred up before the Throne of His Glory.

Pirkei Hekhalot

THE HORSES upon which they ride stand beside mangers of fire, full of coals of juniper, and they eat fiery coals from the mangers, taking a measure of forty bushels of coals in one mouthful.

Pirkei Hekhalot

WHEN ONE is on a higher level, he can see all the secret deeds of man. He knows and recognizes the adulterer, the murderer, and the one who is only suspected of these things. All this he knows and recognizes.

Hekhalot Rabbati

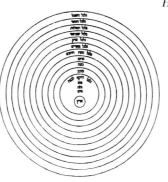

GOD'S NAMES

FIRST BEGIN by combining the letters of the name YHVH. Gaze at all its combinations. Elevate it. Turn it over like a wheel that goes round and round, backwards and forwards like a scroll ... Now begin to combine a few of many letters, to permute and to combine them until your heart is warm. Then be mindful of their movements and of that you can bring forth by moving them. And when you feel that your heart is already warm and when you see that by combinations of letters you can grasp new things, which by human tradition or by yourself you would not be able to know, and when you are thus prepared to receive the influx of divine power which flows into you, then turn all true thoughts to imagine His exalted angels in your heart as if they were human beings sitting or standing about you.

ABRAHAM ABULAFIA

YOU SHOULD constantly keep the letters of the unique name in your mind as if they were in front of you, written in a book with the Torah script. Each letter should appear infinitely large. When you depict the letters of the unique name in this fashion, your mind's eye should gaze on them, and simultaneously your heart should be directed toward the Infinite Being. Your gazing and thought should be as one.

ISAAC OF ACCO

YOU HAVE asked me, my brother, beloved of my soul, to enlighten you regarding the path involving God's names so that through them you will gain what you wish and reach what you desire ... if one wishes to attain what he desires through the use of God's names, he must first study the Torah with all his might.

JOSEPH GIKATILLA

MAN ILLUMINES the world with the light of the divine Name, revealing it from its concealment, thus transforming darkness to light.

SHNEUR ZALMAN OF LIADY

YOU ARE taught that by comprehending the holy names in their respective categories and the appellatives deriving from each, you will realize that everything hinges on His great name, praised be He, and you will yearn to cleave to Him, and you will be in fear and awe of Him.

JOSEPH GIKATILLA

THERE WAS also a name of forty-two letters known among them. Every intelligent person knows that one word of forty-two letters is impossible. But it was a phrase of several words which had together forty-two letters. There is no doubt that the words had such a meaning as to convey a correct notion of the essence of God.

MOSES MAIMONIDES

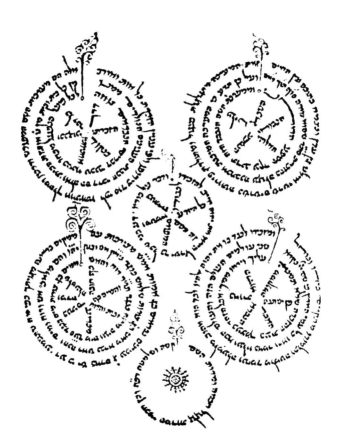

MANY BELIEVE that the forty-two letters are merely to be pronounced mechanically; that by the knowledge of these, without any further interpretation, they can attain to those exalted ends.

MOSES MAIMONIDES

WHENEVER YOU offer your prayers and whenever you study, have the intention of unifying a divine name in every word and with every utterance of your lips.

BAAL SHEM TOV

WHEN A person contemplates the names, he will find that the entire Torah and all the commandments depend on them. If one knows the meaning of all these names, he will understand the greatness of He who spoke and brought the universe into being.

JOSEPH GIKATALIA

APPRECIATE THAT whoever knows the name of God has the spirit of God, the holy spirit, within him.

ABRAHAM ABULAFIA

ONE CAN attach his thoughts to God, and when one does so consistently, there is no question that he will be worthy of the World to Come, and God's Name will be with him constantly, both in this world and in the next.

ISAAC OF ACCO

NEVER UTTER the names without concentration but sanctify them, know them, and reflect that they are the angels of all being and the angels of God sent to you in order to raise you higher and higher and elevate you over all the nations upon earth.

ABRAHAM ABULAFIA

WE KNOW by a prophetic divine tradition of the Torah that when the sage who is an adept combines the letters of the divine name one with the other, the holy spirit flows upon him.

ABRAHAM ABULAFIA

THE NAME of forty-two letters can only be entrusted by us to a person who is modest and meek, in the midway of life, not easily provoked to anger, temperate, and free from vengeful feelings. Whoever understands it, is cautious with it, keeps it in purity, is loved above and is liked here below. He is revered by his fellows; he is heir to two worlds – this world and the world to come.

Talmud

ALPHABET

WHEN YOU look at these holy letters in truth and reliance and when you combine them – placing that which is at the beginning at the end and that which is in the middle at the beginning and that which is at the end and so forth in like manner – these letters will all roll backwards and fowards with many melodies.

ABRAHAM ABULAFIA

I HAVE EXPLAINED what you need to do this, and you lack nothing. Take the pen, parchment and ink, and write the letters, permuting them in such a manner as to denote good. 'Depart from evil, do good, seek peace and pursue it.' (Psalm 34:15)

ABRAHAM ABULAFIA

THE WAY of permutations is the closest way to truly know God.

ABRAHAM ABULAFIA

M ANIPULATE THE letters, and seek out other words having the same numerical value.

ABRAHAM ABULAFIA

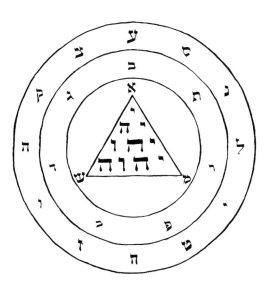

UNITY

YOU MUST include yourself in God's unity, which is the imperative existence. You cannot be worthy of this, however, unless you first nullify yourself.

NAHMAN OF BRATSLAV

HE BRINGS everything from potentiality into actuality, and He varies His deeds, but there is no variety in Him.

Zohar

HE WISHED to make Himself known by His attributes, by each attribute separately. So He let Himself be styled as the God of pardon, the God of justice, the God omnipotent, the God of hosts, and He who is. His object was to make thus intelligible what are His qualities and how His justice and His compassion extend over the world as well as over the works of men.

Zohar

HE IS the beginning as well as the end of all stages; upon Him are stamped all the stages. But He can only be called one, in order to show that although He possesses many forms, he is nothing other than one.

Zohar

THE MAN who knows how to unify the holy name in the correct manner preserves the nation that is unique on earth.

Zohar

IF A MAN comes to unify the holy name and does not do so sincerely and with concentration, but appears in order to promote blessing in the upper and lower worlds, his prayer is rejected and they all proclaim evil against him.

Zohar

WHEN IS 'union' said of man?
When he is male together with female
And is highly sanctified and
Zealous for sanctification.
Then, and only then,
Is he designated 'one',
Without any flaw of any kind.

Hence a man and his wife
Should have a single inclination
At the hour of their union.
The man should rejoice with his wife,
Attaching himself to her with affection,
So joined they make one soul and one body.
A single soul through their affection.
A single body –
For only when male and female are joined
Do they form a single body.

Zohar

ONE MUST direct his heart and will in order to bring blessings above and below … One who seeks to unite the holy name but does not direct his heart, will and awe, in order to grace above and below with blessings, will have his prayers thrown out and evil will be pronounced upon him … But for one who knows how to unite the Holy Name properly, the walls of darkness are split and the king's countenance is revealed and seen by all. When this occurs, everything above and below is blessed.

Zohar

THE PERSON who offers his prayer and unites the holy name properly draws the strand of mercy upon himself. He looks up to the heavens and the light of enlightenment of divine knowledge shines down upon him and crowns him; all stand in awe of him.

Zohar

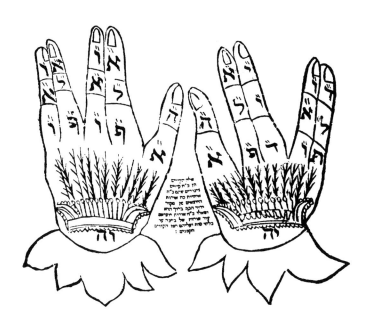

WHEN A person wishes to unify the blessed holy one and His divine presence, he must banish all other thoughts.

Zohar

GOD IS like the ocean
for the waters of the ocean
cannot be grasped and have no shape
except when they are channelled into a vessel,
such as the land,
and taken on a shape;
then we are able to measure them:
the source, the waters of the ocean are one;
then a tributary comes forth
and is channelled into a round basin ...
the source is one
and the channel which comes from it is two.
Next, a large vessel is formed,
as if one dug a large basin
which becomes filled by the waters of the channel;
this becomes three.

Zohar

THIS IS the mystery of the unification. The individual who is worthy of the World to Come must unify the name of the blessed holy one. He must unify the upper and lower levels and limbs, uniting them all and bringing them all to the necessary place, where the knot can be bound.

Zohar

IN EVERY ritual action, let your effort be directed toward uniting the Holy One, blessed be He, and His *Shekhinah* (Divine Presence) through all camps above and below.

Zohar

THE ANCIENTS' statement about unity is an affirmation of perfect oneness. Their statement obligates every person who is perfect in his belief in God's unity and every person who is enlightened concerning unity to make three explicit negations, and they are the negations of corporeality, composition and change in God.

Sefer Maarekhet ha-Elohut

THE BASES of belief are the negations which ought to be made in reference to God for the sake of the perfection of His unity and the proper sequence in which one makes these negations. Everyone following our religion ought to believe that God is one and unique in absolute unity.

Sefer Maarekhet ha-Elohut

GOD IS one, there is no boundary to His wisdom, no measure to His understanding, no limit to His power, and no end to His unity. He has no beginning and no end. The shaper of all and the knower of all has neither front nor back, height nor depth, for He has neither boundary nor end in all that He has. The creator of the world has neither limits nor limbs.

ELEAZAR BEN JUDAH OF WORMS

THE SPIRITUAL union is analogous to the physical union between husband and wife.

MENAHEM MENDEL OF CHERNOBYL

ASCETICISM

A SAGE ONCE came to one of the meditators and asked that he be accepted into their society. The other replied, 'My son, blessed are you to God. Your intentions are good. But tell me, have you attained stoicism?' The sage said, 'Master, explain your words.' The meditator said, 'If one man is praising you and another is insulting you, are the two equal in your eyes or not?' He replied, 'No, my master, I have pleasure from those who praise me, and pain from those who degrade me. But I do not take revenge or bear a grudge.' The other said, 'Go in peace my son. You have not attained stoicism. You have not reached a level where your soul does not feel the praise of one who honours you, nor the degradation of one who insults you. You are not prepared for your thoughts to bound on high, that you should come and meditate.

ISAAC OF ACCO

AN INDIVIDUAL must not afflict himself with fasting lest he become dependent on others.

Sefer Hasidim

A PERSON WHOSE evil passion gains ascendency over him may fast to humble his passion.

Sefer Hasidim

I T IS well known that God created in us a will different from His own in order to subject our will to His. In this He finds satisfaction. This would be impossible unless our will is different from His. When we annihilate our existence, we are connected with the hidden.

HAYYIM HAYKL OF AMDUR

T HE SAGES who were worthy of such undertakings would pray and purify themselves of all uncleanliness. They would fast, immerse in the *mikvah* [ritual bath] and purify themselvs. Then they would make use of various names and gaze into the chambers on high.

HANANEL BEN HUSHIEL

WHEN A person fasts he must be careful not to show anger that day, for fasting makes a person irritable and it is preferable for a person to be satisfied and at peace with people, and not quarrelsome, than to indulge in fasts.

Sefer Hasidim

HE SHOULD not concern himself with the affairs of this world but try in all matters to detach himself from the physical.

BAAL SHEM TOV

A PERSON SHOULD efface himself altogether, with total abandon, both body and soul, to be ready for obliteration in sanctification of God's name, praised be He, both in this world and in the hereafter.

MENAHEM MENDEL OF VITEBSK

TAKE CARE never to speak an unnecessary word, whether by day or by night.

JOSEPH CARO

WHEN A person reaches the attribute of Nothingness, he realizes that he himself is nothing since God grants him existence.

LEVI YITZHAK OF BERDICHEV

ONE OF the great recommendations for one who wishes to know God is that he should be among those who are 'insulted but do not insult'.

ISAAC OF ACCO

'I HAVE BEEN stoic, God is before me at all times' (Psalm 16:8). This denotes a level of stocism with regard to all that befalls a person. Whether people insult Him or praise Him, it should all be equal.

BAAL SHEM TOV

HE SHOULD see to it now he is yet alive so that he can attain this state, namely the stripping away of the corporeality of this world from himself so that only the spiritual remains. Then he will become attached to the worlds on high and be saved from the evil inclination that causes him to sin.

KALONYMUS KALMAN EPSTEIN

YOU SHOULD also mortify your flesh so as to have the merit of seeing Elijah face to face while you are yet awake. He will speak to you mouth to mouth and will greet you, since he will become your teacher in order to teach you all the mysteries of the Torah.

JOSEPH CARO

CLEAVING TO GOD

I T SHOULD be of indifference to him if he be considered a person of little knowledge or as one who is knowledgeable in the entire Torah. The means for attaining this is cleaving to God, for the preoccupation with cleaving to God leaves one no time to think of such matters.

BAAL SHEM TOV

H IS THOUGHTS should cleave to the heavenly realm, and he should not eat or drink to excess, nor seek pleasures.

BAAL SHEM TOV

A T TIMES a person may be engaged in conversation with people, and then he cannot study, but he should still cultivate his attachment to God and focus his mind on God's unity.

BAAL SHEM TOV

MAKE READY to direct the heart to God alone. Cleanse the body and choose a lonely house where no one shall hear your voice. Sit there in your closet and do not reveal your secret to any person. If you can, do it by day in the house, but it is best if you complete it during the night. In the hour when you prepare to speak with the Creator and wish Him to reveal His might to you, then be careful to abstract all thought from the vanities of the world.

ABRAHAM ABULAFIA

COMMIT YOUR works to the Lord and your plans will be established.

BAAL SHEM TOV

THIS IS the purpose for which we have come into the world, to become bound to Him, blessed be He, even if it be only for a moment.

AARON ROTH

WHEN A person attaches himself to God, then all the worlds below him are united with God through him. In this way a person who is endowed with vitality through eating and wearing clothes includes in himself the inanimate, vegetable, animal and rational life; they are all united with God through him.

SHLOMO OF LUTSK

A MAN MUST cause his will and his soul to cleave to his Master and not appear before Him with a deceitful mind, since it is written, 'He that speaks falsehood shall not be established before my eyes' (Psalm 101:7).

Zohar

'TRUST IN the Lord for ever, for the Lord is God, Rock of worlds' (Isa. 26:4). 'Trust in the Lord.' All the world's inhabitants need to strengthen themselves through the Holy One, blessed be He, and to place their trust in Him.

Zohar

H IS HEART should always be joyful, attached to God, no matter what happens.

ISAAC OF ACCO

Y OU MUST respect God and be careful not to attach your thoughts to Him when you are not in a clean place.

ISAAC OF ACCO

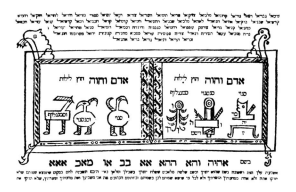

COSMIC REPAIR

I T IS from below that the movement starts, and thereafter is all perfected. If the community of Israel failed to initiate the impulse, the One above would also not move to go to her. It is thus the yearning from below which brings about the completion above.

Zohar

W HAT IS the meaning of elevating the sparks? When you see something corporeal and do not find it to be evil, heaven forbid, you can worship the creator, may He be blessed. For in this thing you can find love or awe or other qualities by which you can elevate it.

LEVI ISAAC OF BERDICHEV

T HE ACT of purification is attained through raising oneself, with the element of the divine that inheres in one, toward the source of all, toward God.

MENAHEM MENDEL OF CHERNOBYL

I HEARD A convincing argument said in the name of my teacher the Baal Shem Tov. It concerned the strange thoughts which come to a man in the midst of his prayer. They come from the mystery of the broken vessels and the 288 sparks which need to be clarified every day. They appear in order to be repaired and elevated. The strange thought which appears one day is different from that of another day. The Baal Shem Tov taught that one must pay close attention to this matter. I learned from him how to repair the strange throughts even if they are thoughts about women. One should elevate them and make them cleave to their source, the *sefirah* [divine emanation] *Hesed* [Mercy].

JACOB JOSEPH OF POLONNOYE

A PERSON MUST purify himself, to remove from himself his 'filth' so that his grossness will not impede him from seeing the brightness of the Torah.

MENAHEM MENDEL OF CHERNOBYL

SOUL

MAN IS endowed with a divine soul which distinguishes him from creatures below him, but he must not deceive himself that he actually possesses this distinction.

JUDAH LOEW OF PRAGUE

I THINK THAT God alone gives men pure good health which is not preceded by any disease in the body; but that health which is an escape from disease He gives through the medium of skill and medical science. It is attributed to science and whoever can apply it skilfully, even though in truth it is God Himself who heals both by these means and without these means. The same is the case with regard to the soul – the good things, namely, food, He gives to men by His power alone, but those which contain in them a deliverance from evil He gives by means of His angels and His word.

PHILO OF ALEXANDRIA

THE AIR is the habitation of incorporeal souls because it seemed good to the Creator of the universe to fill all parts of the world with living creatures ... Not only is it not deserted by all things, besides, it is rather like a populous city, full of imperishable and immortal citizens, souls equal in number to the stars. Now regarding these souls, some descend upon the earth so as to be bound up in mortal bodies ... others soar upwards ... while others condemning the body to be a great folly and trifling, have pronounced it a prison and a grave. Flying from it as from a house of correction or a tomb, they have raised themselves aloft on light wings towards the aether, devoting their whole lives to sublime speculations. Again there are others – the purest and most excellent of all – who possess greater and more divine intellects and never by any chance desire any earthly thing whatever.

PHILO OF ALEXANDRIA

SEEKING TO mine the wealth of his own soul, he found there the soul of the universe.

ARIEL BENSION

THE SOUL descended from its glorious abode and became robed in the physical, so that no matter what noble spiritual perceptions she reaches, once robed in the physical, these perceptions are all subject to the limitations of time and space.

SHNEUR ZALMAN OF LIADY

EACH ONE suffers according to the state of his soul and the level of his service to God.

NAHMAN OF BRATSLAV

THERE IS a field, where trees and plants of indescribable beauty grow. Fortunate is the eye that has seen this. The trees and plants – these are holy souls in a state of ascending.

NAHMAN OF BRATSLAV

misit:
Ceadi
sui qu
uic·m
consul
uiuer
Ange
thesos
occur
& dice
misit

WHEN, OUT of great darkness of soul and blockage and distress, the Holy One, blessed be He, brings illumination to man, he then begins to long for God, blessed be He.

AARON ROTH

IT FOLLOWS that in proportion to the degree of engagement by a person in this world, so is the flow of divine grace to his soul.

AARON ROTH

AS LONG as the holy soul cleaves to a man, he is beloved by his master. Many guardians protect him on all sides. He is noted for good both above and below, and the holy *Shekhinah* [divine presence] dwells with him. But when he perverts his ways, the *Shekhinah* leaves him, and the holy soul no longer cleaves to him.

Zohar

WHEN A person's soul yearns to serve the Creator and when the Lord of the Manor observes his longing, that person can be spiritually elevated.

AARON ROTH

THE DIVINE influx will begin to prevail in you, and will weaken your external and internal organs. Your entire body will begin to tremble, until you think that you are about to die. This is because your soul is separating itself from your body as a result of the great joy that you experience when you perceive and recognize these things.

ABRAHAM ABULAFIA

THERE IS no question that if a person is a saint, and is perfect in all his deeds, then his soul will ascend on high each night.

HAYYIM VITAL

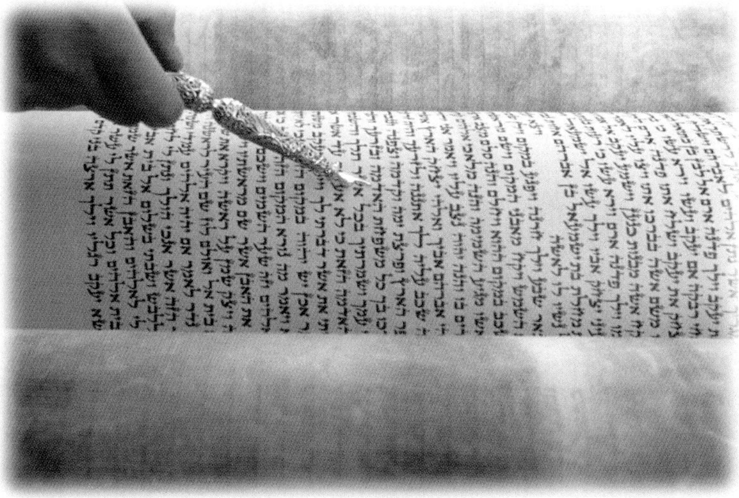

STUDY

A PERSON SHOULD not say, 'I will study the Bible so people will call me a scholar. I will study *Mishnah* so people will call me Master. I will study *Talmud* so that I be deemed a sage and sit in the academy.' Rather he should study out of love.

BAHYA IBN PAKUDA

M Y MASTER, of blessed memory, told me that a person's prime intention when studying Torah should be to bring enlightenment and the highest holiness to himself.

HAYYIM VITAL

I T IS also important to have a set order of study each day and not miss it.

HAYYIM VITAL

THEN HE is to perfect his life by performing positive commandments and by directing his prayers towards their highest purpose; by zealously studying the Torah for its own sake as an ox bows its head to the yoke until his strength is sapped; by confining himself to few pleasures, eating and drinking little; by rising at midnight or a little earlier; by turning away from all unbecoming traits; and by withdrawing from people, even from idle conversation.

HAYYIM VITAL

THEY OCCUPY themselves deeply in the study of the Torah or in prayer with such great, burning enthusiasm that they experience the fragrance and sweetness of God.

KALONYMOUS KALMAN EPSTEIN

LUST CAN take the form of inspiring a person avidly to study the Torah and to serve God, and with like avidity to pursue all the commandments.

MENAHEM MENDEL OF CHERNOBYL

THE CREATOR opened for us three gates for the knowledge of his Torah and his law: the first is the sound mind; the second is the text of Torah revealed to his prophet Moses; and the third is the traditions we have received from early masters which were transmitted to them by the prophets.

BAHYA IBN PAKUDA

THE *KABBALAH* that eludes most rabbis who concentrate on talmudic study is generally divided into two parts. The first deals with knowing God through the method of the ten *sefirot* [divine emanations] called 'plants', so that whoever effects disunity among the *sefirot* is guilty of cutting down the plants – it is the *sefirot* that manifest the secret of divine unity. The other part involves knowing God through the method of the twenty-two letters of the alphabet ... These two methods are not perceived through the senses, nor known as axioms, nor are they part of commonly accepted knowledge.

ABRAHAM ABULAFIA

BLESSED ARE those who study the Torah in order to know the wisdom of their master, and who know and understand the supernal mysteries, for when a man leaves the world in this way, all punishments in the world are removed from him.

Zohar

THE BOUNDARY of truth and the tradition of the covenant is this. If one wishes to attain what he desires through the use of God's names, he must first study the Torah with all his might, so that he can grasp the meaning of every one of God's names mentioned in the Torah.

JOSEPH GIKATILLA

PERFECTION

THE FIRST perfection is self-fulfilment; the second is the perfection of this world; the third is the perfection of the upper world and all its heavenly hosts; and the fourth is the perfection of the divine name.

Zohar

IT IS not that he fears punishment in this world or in the next but rather he is afraid that he may not be perfect before God whom he loves.

ELEAZAR BEN JUDAH OF WORMS

THE DIFFERENCES between man and higher beings are that the higher beings are in a state of perfection and they do not need to bring their potentialities to self-realization.

JUDAH LOEW OF PRAGUE

Know that an individual may at times be perfected through impregnation and at times he may require reincarnation, which is more painful.

Jacob Zemah

If a person has not perfected himself by fulfilling all the 613 commandments in action, speech and thought, he will be subject to reincarnation.

Jacob Zemah

PRAYER

WHEN YOU pray, recite your prayers to the tune of a melody that is pleasant and agreeable to you ... and then you will pray with devotion and your heart will be drawn after the utterance of your lips.

Sefer Hasidim

MAN, IN SO far as he is a physical being, is not one with God. Therefore, when he comes before God in prayer, he must shed all bodily attributes, as though he is wholly spiritual.

JUDAH LOEW OF PRAGUE

SO PRAYER is made up of both action and speech; when the action is faulty, speech does not find a spot to rest in. Such prayer is not prayer, and the man offering it is defective in the upper world and the lower.

Zohar

THE FIRST method is that on that particular day, the individual should have perfect intention in his prayers ... such an individual can certainly have his soul rise at night, ascending to 'God's mountain, His holy place'.

HAYYIM VITAL

WHENEVER YOU offer prayers and whenever you study, have the intention of unifying a divine name in every word and with every utterance of your lips, for there are worlds, souls and divinity in every letter.

BAAL SHEM TOV

ONCE HE has ministered to the sages, studied Torah and offered up many supplications, he will be worthy of offering pure prayer. Then illumination will come to him from on high in order that he will truly be able to make petitions with a stripping away of corporeality.

KALONYMUS KALMAN EPSTEIN

THE ROOT of prayer is that the heart rejoices in the love of the Holy One, blessed be He.

ELEAZAR BEN JUDAH OF WORMS

TAKE CARE to have no other thought in mind during your prayers except the actual words of the prayers, not even thoughts of the Torah and the precepts.

JOSEPH CARO

NOT ALL tears find their way to the king. Tears of anger and tears of accusation against one's fellow do not come into the king's presence. But tears of repentance and prayer do, as well as the tears of those who ask for relief from their distress.

Zohar

SIT IN the synagogue with awe and trembling.

HAYYIM VITAL

EVERYTHING IN the world depends on the repentance and prayer that a man offers to the Holy One, blessed be He. And this is even more true if a man weeps while he prays, for there is no gate that those tears cannot penetrate.

Zohar

A MAN WHO is praying should make himself poor, so that his prayer may enter with the generality of the poor, for all the gatekeepers allow the poor to enter far more easily than anyone else, for they enter even without asking permission. And if a man makes himself poor and adopts the approach of a poor man, his prayer ascends and meets the prayers of the poor, and joins them and ascends with them, and it enters as one of them and is received willingly by the holy king.

Zohar

DO NOT worry about anything in the world, other than that which will influence your worship of God.

JOSEPH CARO

SPIRITUAL MASTER

For all that you see of the way the *zaddikim* [spiritual masters] serve the Lord in public is no more than a drop in the ocean compared with their inner life.

ELIMELECH OF LYZHANSK

There are amongst them such *zaddikim* [spiritual masters] as are capable of virtually raising the dead through the power of their prayer.

ZECHARIAH MENDEL OF JAROSLAW

The incomplete *zaddik* [spiritual master] does not hate the source of evil with an absolute hatred and therefore he does not show absolute contempt for the evil deed; and because his hate and contempt for these is not absolute, there remains a lingering of some love for them and some craving for their pleasures.

SHNEUR ZALMAN OF LIADY

EOPLE FIND it difficult to understand why one must travel to the master in order to hear the teaching from his lips because, as they see it, one can study moralistic works. But this is of great value, for there is a great difference between hearing the truth from the master directly, and hearing it quoted by others in his name.

NAHMAN OF BRATSLAV

F HE sits at the feet of his teacher and knows of a certain problem and appreciates that his teacher or his companion knows of it too, let him allow them to ask and he should remain silent. If they do not ask, he should say, 'So-and-so asks this, and he gave this reply', and he should pay honour to his companion and not take any credit for himself ... A further mark of humility is that a man should always give precedence to his neighbour's name before his own ... he should always state his neighbour's reasoning before his own. To sum it all up, he should decrease as far as he possibly can his own honour but increase the honour of those who fear the Lord.

ELEAZER BEN JUDAH OF WORMS

ONE MUST seek out a true leader and draw close to him, for every true leader partakes of the spirit of prophecy.

NAHMAN OF BRATSLAV

THE TRUE *zaddik* [spiritual master] proceeds in his prayers through all the upper worlds until he reaches the Supernal Intelligences, and from there he proceeds until he reaches *Ayn Sof*.

KALONYMUS KALMAN EPSTEIN

THE WAY of the *zaddikim* [spiritual masters] who walk in the way of the Lord is well known. They occupy themselves mightily in the study of the Torah or in prayer with such great burning enthusiasm, as they experience the fragrance and sweetness of God, blessed be He, that it would take but little for them to become annihilated out of existence in their great longing to become attached to God's divinity, as they ascend from heavenly hall to heavenly hall and from spiritual world to spiritual world.

KALONYMUS KALMAN EPSTEIN

EVEN WHEN the *zaddikim* [spiritual masters] converse with other human beings their thoughts soar aloft towards the exaltedness of God, and they perform various unifications.

ELIMELECH OF LYZHANSK

WHEN THEY [the spiritual masters] study the holy *Gemara* (*Talmud*), fire actually consumes them, so great is their love and holiness.

ELIMELECH OF LYZHANSK

MEDITATION

MY MASTER also said that it is good for a person to live in a house with windows open to the heavens so that he can always lift his eyes to the heavens and gaze at them.

HAYYIM VITAL

HE SHOULD isolate himself for periods of time and contemplate the fear of God.

HAYYIM VITAL

WHEN YOU meditate and express your spontaneous thoughts before God, you can be worthy of nullifying all desires and all evil traits.

NAHMAN OF BRATSLAV

YOU MUST therefore be alone, at night, on an isolated path, where people are not usually found. Go there and meditate, cleansing your heart and mind of all worldy affairs.

NAHMAN OF BRATSLAV

THE MAIN time to meditate is at night. This is a time when the world is free from mundane concerns.

NAHMAN OF BRATSLAV

MAKE YOURSELF ready to meet your God, O Israel. Get ready to turn your heart to God alone, cleanse your body, and choose a special place where none will hear you, and remain altogether by yourself in isolation.

ABRAHAM ABULAFIA

BE ALONE one hour each day, to take stock of yourself.

MORDECAI OF CHERYNOBL

IT IS of the greatest importance to practice a regular period of withdrawal.

NAHMAN OF BRATSLAV

WHEN A person does not reflect on the real purpose of his life, what meaning is there to his existence?

NAHMAN OF BRATSLAV

CONSTANTLY MEDITATE on the Divine Presence.

BAAL SHEM TOV

IF ONE has the power to endure the way of rebuke with great passion, and if his mind can control its fantasies, then he can ride his mind like a horse. He can control it as he desires, spurring it on to go forward, or reigning it to stop where he pleases.

ABRAHAM ABULAFIA

TAKE IN your hand a scribe's pen. Write speedily, letting your tongue utter the words with a pleasant melody, very slowly. Understand the words that leave your lips. The words can consist of anything that you desire, in any language that you desire, for you must return all languages to their original substance.

ABRAHAM ABULAFIA

MEDITATE IN a state of rapture so as to receive the divine influx.

ABRAHAM ABULAFIA

'PREPARE TO meet your God, O Israel. Prepare yourself, unify your heart, and purify your body. Choose a special place for yourself, where your voice will not be heard by anyone else. Meditate alone, with no one else present. Sit in one place in a room or attic. Do not reveal your secret to anyone.

ABRAHAM ABULAFIA

PREPARE YOUR innner thoughts to depict God and His highest angels. Depict them in your heart as if they were human beings, sitting or standing around you. You are in their midst, like a messenger whom the King and his servants wish to send on a mission. You are ready to hear the words of the message, whether it is from the King or from one of His servants, from His mouth, or from the mouth of any one of them.

ABRAHAM ABULAFIA

THE TRUE path is straight, depending on the concentration of the individual. He must know how to concentrate on its truth with attachment of thought and desire, derived from its unfathomable power.

The Gate of Kavanah

ONE WHO is worthy to reach the level of meditation has peace in this life.

ISAAC OF ACCO

G O AND increase the humbleness of your heart, and learn to treat everything equally until you have become stoic. Only then will you be able to meditate.

ISAAC OF ACCO

FEAR OF GOD

'LET A man always be subtle in the fear of God.' This means that a person should reflect on the subtleties and the glories of the world: how, for example, a mortal king commands his soldiers to engage in battle. Even though they know they may be killed, they are afraid of him and obey him even though they know that the fear of him is not everlasting, because he will eventually die and perish and they can escape to another country. How much more so, therefore, should men fear the King of the King of Kings, the Holy One, blessed be He, and walk in His ways, since He is everywhere and gazes at the wicked as well as the good.

ELEAZAR BEN JUDAH OF WORMS

THE FEAR of God is not of punishment in the hereafter; it is not motivated by a desire for benefits in this world or the next, but it is a fear lest one not be wholly devoted to the love of the Creator, praised be He.

Sefer Hasidim

THE BASIS of hasidic piety is the fear of God, which is shown when a person lusts for some pleasure and he ignores his temptation out of the fear of God.

Sefer Hasidim

THE ROOT of the fear of the Lord is when a man desires something yet he gives up the pleasure for which his evil inclination craves because he fears the Lord.

ELEAZAR BEN JUDAH OF WORMS

ONE IN whose heart there is the fear of God will certainly consider not to lose a permanent world that lasts for ever because of a world that passes away. He will certainly be ready to suffer torture and death for an hour in this lowly and despicable world and acquire thereby the world on high, which endures for ever and ever.

ALEXANDER SUSSKIND

'THE SECRET of the Lord is with them that fear Him', that is today, for them it always remains an incommunicable secret since the more God-fearing a man is the less capable is he of revealing the secrets of his heart.

KALONYMUS KALMAN EPSTEIN

LOVE OF GOD

LOVING HIM means that the love of God be so firmly fixed in a person's heart that it ever inspires him to please Him.

MOSES HAYYIM LUZZATTO

'LET HIM kiss me with the kisses of his mouth' (Songs of Songs 1:2). What did King Solomon mean by introducing words of love between the upper world and the lower world, and by beginning the praise of love, which he has introduced between them, with 'let him kiss me'? They have already given an explanation for this, and it is that inseparable love of spirit for spirit can be expressed only by a kiss, and a kiss is with the mouth, for that is the source and outlet of the spirit. And when they kiss one another, the spirits cling to each other, and they are one, and then love is one.

Zohar

LOVER WHO is not jealous – his love is not love. When he becomes jealous, his love is complete. Hence we learn that a man needs to be jealous of his wife, so that he may bind himself to her in perfect love, for as a result he will not glance at another woman.

Zohar

THE ROOT of love is to love the Lord.

ELEAZAR BEN JUDAH OF WORMS

HAVE NO other thought in your mind than your love.

BAAL SHEM TOV

HOW DOES the Holy One, blessed be He, reprove someone? He reproves him with love, in secret.

Zohar

THE DISCLOSURE of the divine must be 'with all your heart'.

SHNEUR ZALMAN OF LIADY

A PERSON SHOULD serve God with all his strength, for all our faculties are intended for God's service.

BAAL SHEM TOV

GLORY

SWEET MELODIES will I sing to you
And hymns compose,
For my soul yearns for your presence
To know the mystery of your being.
When I but bring your praises to my lips
My love for you wells up within my heart;
Therefore will I extol you
And honour your name with songs of adoration.
I will tell of your glory
Though I have not seen you;
I will speak of you in similes
Though I cannot know your essence.
You revealed a semblance of your splendour
In the mystic visions of your faithful servants, the
    prophets.
They envisioned your grandeur and your might
From the stupendous work of your creation.
They speak of you not as you are
By inference from your handiwork.
They portrayed you in countless forms
That are all but imperfect aspects of your oneness.
They envisioned you as a sage and as a youth;

As a sage sitting in judgement
And as a youth in the day of battle,
As a warrior staking his strength in combat,
Wearing the helmet of victory on his head,
Defeating his foes by his right arm, by his holy might.
I will proclaim his renown,
For he has conferred his love on me,
And he will be to me a crown of splendour.
I see his head luminous as pure gold,
His holy name inscribed upon his forehead.
Adorned by his people with a crown
Of grace and glory, magnificence and beauty.
O may the temple of righteousness,
His noble ornament,
Be remembered in his favour,
May he keep his beloved people in glory,
Crowned with the sovereign diadem of beauty.
His splendour is my renown, and mine is his,
And he is near to me when I call on him.
He revealed the ways of his providence
To his humble servant Moses,
Who glimpsed the fullness of his eternal mystery.
He loves his people,
His humble seed he glorifies,

He who is surrounded by man's praise
Takes delight in them.
The essence of your word is truth;
O you who have called into being the generations
Extend your care to a people that yearns for you.
Receive the multitude of my hymns,
And may the song of my prayer come before you.
Let my prayer be like incense,
Let a poor man's song be to you
As the song once chanted at the altar of sacrifice.
May my prayer come before you,
The sustainer of the universe and its creator,
The just, the mighty one.
Accept the silent promptings of my heart,
For all my being is astir with longing for your
    presence.

HASIDEI ASHKENAZ

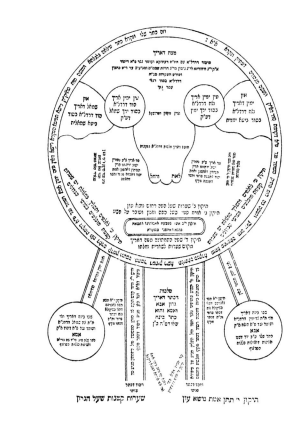

רעותין וכוליה מ"א ז

ראש מחר שלו וקוקמ מחר שללא בגולגלתא

מנח דאריך

יסוד דרדל"א עם תחלת רעותיה ועומד נגד פ"א דיושר
אלקין אחזחרא לי"נ נישן מ"ד חיות שבם"ם וזמ"ע"ס עד ריש כתפין
ותורע הטענחת פנ"א
דרדל"א בסוד רגל
עמר נקי

<table>
<tr><td>אין
שמאל דאריך
סוד דרדלי"ח כסוד
בית שמאלות</td><td>עין ימין דאריך
סוד דרדלי"ח
כסוד יך שמאל
דע"ק</td><td></td><td>עין ימין דאריך
גלח דרדלי"ח
כסוד יך ימין
דע"ק</td><td>אין
ימין דאריך
גלח דרדלי"ח
כסוד גיצת ימים</td></tr>
</table>

חטם דאריך מלוח דרדל"א בגבורות

היקון ל' שערות שעל פטל רחום ותתא חון
תיקון ג' מוחא ספרי כטל כפם ותתן ושוכר על פשע

תיקון רי"ב שתו נשבעה לאבותינו ותשבא
טובינ דאהבני משערות

היקון ד' שטרו בתחתונוב מסת דאריך
מקום שערות לשתרות מלתא

<table>
<tr><td></td><td>סלתה
דכתר דאריך
גרון אבא
ואמא והוא
כתר בנח
שלי"ח רס"ח ה"ב ן</td><td></td></tr>
</table>

רסוד דכתר

שערות קצנות שעל הגרון   תיקון י' תתן אמת טשא און

KING OF the kings, God of Gods, and Lord of Lords,
Who is surrounded with chains of crowns,
Who is encompassed by the cluster of the rulers of
    radiance,
Who covers the heavens with the wing of His
    magnificence,
And in His majesty appeared from the heights,
And from His stature the heavens are sparked.
His stature sends out the lofty,
And His crown blazes out the mighty,
And His garment flows with the precious.
And all trees shall rejoice in His word,
And herbs shall exult in His rejoicing,
And His words shall drop as perfumes,
Flowing forth in flames of fire,
Giving joy to those who search them,
And quiet to those who fulfil them.

Pirkei Hekhalot

MAJESTY AND faithfulness belong to the eternal God,
Understanding and blessing belong to the eternal God,
Splendour and greatness belong to the eternal God,
Knowledge and communication belong to the eternal God,
Nobility and glory belong to the eternal God,
Decision and firmness belong to the eternal God,
Uprightness and lustre belong to the eternal God,
Might and softness belong to the eternal God,
Adornment and purity belong to the eternal God,
Unity and awe belong to the eternal God,
Crown and glory belong to the eternal God,
Teaching and insight belong to the eternal God,
Dominion and sovereignty belong to the eternal God,
Beauty and victory belong to the eternal God,
Magnificence and strength belong to the eternal God,
Power and gentleness belong to the eternal God,
Redemption and glory belong to the eternal God,
Beauty and righteousness belong to the eternal God,
Summons and sanctity belong to the eternal God,
Jubilation and exaltation belong to the eternal God,
Song and praise belong to the eternal God,
Adulation and eminence belong to the eternal God.

Hekhalot Rabbati

WHILE I am speaking of the great and marvellous holiness of the Torah of our great master, I am reminded of something ... that makes my heart burn as a flaming fire.

HAYYIM OF VOLOZHIN

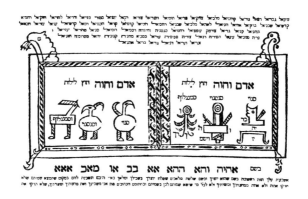

PROPHECY

PROPHECY IS a mode of the intellect. It is the expression of the love of the Lord our God, the Lord is one ... Here is the strong foundation, which I deliver to you that you should know it and embrace it upon your heart: the Holy Name, the whole of the Torah, the sacred Scriptures and all the prophetic books; these are all full of divine names and tremendous things. Join one to the other. Depict them to yourself. Test them, try them, combine them.

ABRAHAM ABULAFIA

WHEN AN individual is worthy of the mystery of attachment to God, he can also be worthy of the mystery of stoicism. After he is worthy of stoicism, he can also be worthy of meditation. And after he is worthy of meditation, he can be worthy of enlightenment. From there he can reach the level of prophecy where he can actually predict the future.

ISAAC OF ACCO

EZEKIEL BEGAN to complain to the Holy One, blessed be He, saying, 'Sovereign of the universe! Am I not a priest and a prophet? Why did Isaiah prophesy in Jerusalem, yet I have to prophesy among the captives? Why did Hosea prophesy in Jerusalem, yet I have to prophesy among the captives? Of Isaiah, it is written, "The vision of Isaiah." If it is because their prophecies brought good tidings and mine evil, it is not so, rather mine are good and theirs were evil.' A parable was told. To what can this be compared? To a king of flesh and blood with many servants whom he allowed tasks to perform. He made the cleverest a shepherd, whereupon that clever man protested, 'My colleagues stay in an inhabited place; why should I have to be in the wilderness?' Similarly, Ezekiel protested. 'All my colleagues were in Jerusalem, why should I have to be among the captives?' No sooner did Ezekiel speak in that fashion than the Holy One, blessed be He, opened seven compartments down below. These are the compartments down below. Ezekiel gazed into these in order to see all that is on high.

Vision of Ezekiel

A JEW CANNOT be as devoted and true to his own ideas, sentiments and imagination in the diaspora as he can in *Eretz Israel*; outside it, they are mixed with dross and much impurity … In the Holy Land man's imagination is lucid and clear, clean and pure, capable of receiving the revelations of divine truth and of expressing in life the sublime meaning of the idea of prophecy and to be illuminated by the radiance of the Holy Spirit.

ABRAHAM ISAAC KOOK

W HEN AN individual completely enters the mystery of prophecy, he suddenly sees his own image standing before him. He becomes totally unaware of his own essence, as if it were concealed from him. Then he sees his own image standing before him, speaking to him, and telling him of the future.

ABRAHAM ABULAFIA

MARTYRDOM

HE SHOULD depict to himself that at this moment they are actually carrying out these forms of death and he should depict the pain and suffering that will be his ... the Creator ... who searches the hearts, sees his thoughts and the manner in which he depicts to himself the deaths and tortures inflicted upon him and yet he survives the test.

ALEXANDER SUSSKIND

REGARDING DEATH by burning, he should imagine that they want to compel him to bow to the image while they have a small pan filled with molten lead over a fire and they say to him, 'Unless you bow down to this image we shall pour this lead down your throat' ... He should imagine how he opens his mouth of his own accord and how they pour the lead down his throat and the terrible sufferings he will endure.

ALEXANDER SUSSKIND

A S A result of this martyrdom, albeit only *in potentia*, in his thoughts, with great rapture and with the intention of sacrificing God's name throughout the worlds, the great name of our Maker and Creator, may He be exalted, is elevated and sanctified in all worlds, by both those on high and those here below.

ALEXANDER SUSSKIND

W HEN THINKING of death by stoning, a man should imagine himself to be standing on the edge of a tower of great height and facing him are many belonging to the nations of the world and with an image in their hands, and they say to him, 'Bow to this image, otherwise we shall throw you off the edge of the tower.' He replies, 'I have no desire to bow to a graven or molten image, the work of men's hands, since our God is called the God of all the earth; He is the God of Israel. He is God in the heavens above and on the earth beneath; there is none else. To him will I bow the knee and prostrate myself.' He should then depict to himself that they cast him from the tower to the ground and he should also dwell on the terrible sufferings that will be his.

ALEXANDER SUSSKIND

HUMAN BEINGS

GOOD

I<small>F A POOR</small> person and an affluent person be sick, and many go to visit the affluent person, one should go to visit the poor one, even if the affluent person is also learned in the Torah.

Sefer Hasidim

O<small>NE SHOULD</small> not be ambitious and greedy for wealth, nor lazy and shrinking from work, but of a generous eye, modestly pursuing his occupation, engage in study of the Torah, take pleasure in the little that is his portion.

Sefer Hasidim

O<small>NE SHOULD</small> shun anger altogether even at the members of his household, and should not show impatience in any degree.

H<small>AYYIM</small> V<small>ITAL</small>

HAPPY THE person who continues in his uprightness to walk in the good path, keeping far from the wicked in those days. Perhaps he will be saved from the troubles known as the birthpangs of the Messiah.

ABRAHAM BEN ISAAC OF GRANADA

ONE SHOULD also avoid idle chatter.

HAYYIM VITAL

THE CHOICEST path is the path followed by the saintly pietists of ancient times. It demands that a person repent with great earnestness all wrongs he has committed.

HAYYIM VITAL

IN WHATEVER act he performs in the service of God, he should consider that he thereby brings delight to his Creator, praised be He.

BAAL SHEM TOV

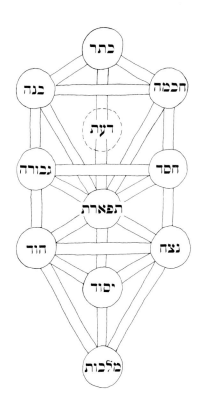

MAN MUST achieve the good, which is his end, thereby justifying his existence, and when his existence has been justified, the whole universe has been justified, since all hinges on man.

JUDAH LOEW OF PRAGUE

THE PERSON who is to rebuke others is under an obligation to rebuke himself for his own offences and to mend his ways before criticizing others – otherwise they will not listen to him.

Sefer Hasidim

ONE MUST be truthful in speech, upright in spirit, and his heart should be free of all perversity and vanity.

Sefer Hasidim

ONE IS not to indulge in excessive joking, nor be overly sad and grieving.

Sefer Hasidim

ONE MUST not desist from rebuking one's neighbour till one turns him to the right course and he desists from offences in worldly matters and in his relationship to God.

Sefer Hasidim

ONE MAY not open a barrel of wine suggesting that he is doing so in the other person's honour when the barrel had to be opened in any case.

Sefer Hasidim

BE GENTLE in your replies to all men.

JOSEPH CARO

ONE MUST judge both litigants equally, and keep far away from anything false, in case people say there is some partiality in the case. For it is said of the Holy One, blessed be He, 'He is not partial, nor does He take bribes' (Deut. 10:17).

Zohar

IT IS not Torah and good deeds, but his intention of doing good which is accounted to a person as something great.

Sefer Hasidim

ONE MUST be a person of integrity in all aspects of his being.

Sefer Hasidim

WHEN HOLY Israelites meet together to encourage one another, the Holy One, blessed be He, gets there first in order to hearken to the holy words they speak.

AARON ROTH

THE MIDDLE course is attainable by every person, and every individual should try to reach it.

SHNEUR ZALMAN OF LIADY

As a person must believe in the Holy One, praised be He, so must he believe in himself.

Zadok HaKohen of Lublin

Even if one has good reason to display his temper, he should avoid it.

Hayyim Vital

Beware against depression whatever may happen.

Mordecai of Chernobyl

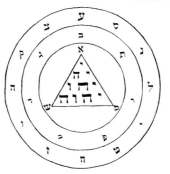

EVIL

D O NOT assume that the need to probe one's ways and turn back from evil applies only to offences involving action, such as robbery or fornication or theft and the like, but as a person must turn back from these, so must he turn back from character traits such as anger, hatred, envy, mocking and lusting after food and the like.

Sefer Hasidim

E VEN A single word of deception is forbidden.

Sefer Hasidim

A PERSON IN whom God created the evil impulse must endeavour to free himself from this passion. And even if one is righteous and pious he must not think to himself that this is an easy task.

JUDAH LOEW OF PRAGUE

THOUGH A person is opposed to Satan, that is, the evil impulse, this opposition in itself will not enable him to prevail, without divine help.

JUDAH LOEW OF PRAGUE

WHEN ONE commences serving God, he must not be overly punctilious about everything he does. This is of the evil impulse's doing to induce fear in a person that he is not doing enough.

MENAHEM MENDEL OF VITEBSK

HE MUST not show partiality to an elder or a person of distinction if he is not to be deemed under censure for failing to rebuke him.

Sefer Hasidim

WHOEVER FAILS to rebuke his neighbour shares in his guilt.

Sefer Hasidim

ONE MUST not be a contentious person, envious and lusting, nor avid for honour, for envy, lust and avidity for honour undermine a person's life in the world.

Sefer Hasidim

ONE SHOULD not be ambitious and greedy for wealth.

Sefer Hasidim

A PERSON MUST devote time and devise a strategy to condition himself to truly despise evil.

SHNEUR ZALMAN OF LIADY

BEWARE OF anger, flattery, falsehood.

MORDECAI OF CHERNOBYL

BE CAREFUL of the company you keep.

MORDECAI OF CHERNOBYL

KNOW THAT there are evildoers who struggle all their lives to uproot themselves altogether from God and His Torah.

NAHMAN OF BRATSLAV

ONE MUST judge each person favourably. Even if a person be completely evil it is necessary to seek and find some good in him.

NAHMAN OF BRATSLAV

WHEN THE evil power comes to seduce man, drag him to the Torah and he will depart from him.

Zohar

DO NOT flatter any person or envy any person.

MORDECAI OF CHERNOBYL

WHEN THE evil power stands before the Holy One, blessed be He, in order to make accusations against the world because of mankind's evil deeds, the Holy One, blessed be He, takes pity on the world and advises mankind how to escape from him, and then he cannot rule either over them or over their deeds.

Zohar

NEVER LOSE your temper over material things.

JOSEPH CARO

MAN'S SERVICE to God consists in overcoming the evil power completely, banishing it from the body, from thought and speech and action.

SHNEUR ZALMAN OF LIADY

JUST AS a man is punished for the evil word that he utters, so is he punished for the good word that he has the opportunity to speak but does not speak.

Zohar

COMMANDMENTS

EVERY *MITZVAH* [commandment] a person can perform should be performed; whatever a person cannot perform, he should think of performing it. This is illustrated by the story of a person who was a shepherd and did not know how to pray. Every day he used to say, 'Sovereign of the universe, you know that if you had cattle to entrust to my care, others would charge for this; but for you I would do it for nothing because I love you.'

Sefer Hasidim

THE NEGATIVE duties of the heart include: that we shall not covet; that we shall not exact vengeance or bear a grudge; that our minds shall not focus on forbidden things, that we lust not after them, that we do not give consent to carry them out; and similar rules which apply to the inner life that none can see except the Creator.

BAHYA IBN PAKUDA

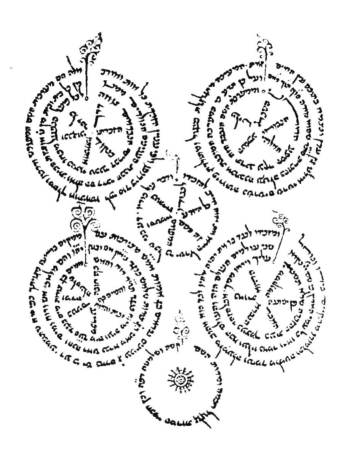

AMONG THE positive commandments in the category of the duties of the heart are: the belief that the world had a Creator; that He created it *ex nihilo*; that there is none like Him; that we are under obligation to acknowledge His unity, to worship Him with our hearts; to contemplate the wonders manifested by His creatures, so that these serve as tokens of His nature; that we trust in Him, humble ourselves before Him, and feel awed by Him; that we feel embarrassed when we realize that He observes our open acts and secret thoughts; that we yearn to please Him; that our conduct be devoted solely to glorifying His name; that we love Him, and love those that love Him in order to be close to Him; that we spurn those who spurn Him.

BAHYA IBN PAKUDA

MAN IS in a state of potentiality, and he was created for self-realization through the study of Torah and the performance of the commandments.

JUDAH LOEW OF PRAGUE

IT IS written in the Torah: 'You shall surely rebuke your neighbour and not bear sin because of him' (Lev. 19:17). This obligates us to rebuke a fellow-Jew who in resignation or laziness fails to perform any of the 248 positive commandments or who violates any of the prescribed negative commandments.

Sefer Hasidim

THE DUTIES of external conduct are two-fold: one consists of rational commandments, which we would be under obligation to carry out even if they were not ordained in the Torah, and the other consists of duties based on traditional prescription, which reason does not demand but neither does it reject.

BAHYA IBN PAKUDA

BE NOT like servants who serve the master so as to receive a reward, but be like servants who serve the master without expecting a reward.

BAHYA IBN PAKUDA

PERFORM GOOD deeds for their own sake, and speak of them as ends in themselves. Do not turn them into a crown with which to adorn yourself, nor a spade to dig with.

BAHYA IBN PAKUDA

OUR SAGES have taught that whoever had the opportunity to chastise any fellow-Jew for violation of a positive or negative commandment and watched resignedly without doing so is deemed culpable for all those offenses.

Sefer Hasidim

EVERY SERVICE performed by a physical act and all commandments which they fulfil have only one objective – to condition the heart to righteousness.

ZADOK HAKOHEN OF LUBLIN

'THOU SHALT not hear a false report' (Exod. 23:1) – not listen to vain words. This is the negative precept. The positive precept is: 'And now, O Israel, harken to the statutes' (Deut. 4:1).

ELEAZAR BEN JUDAH OF WORMS

THE ROOT of saintliness is for a man to go beyond the letter of the law.

ELEAZAR BEN JUDAH OF WORMS

THE WAY in which we bind somethingness to nothingness is by means of the Torah and the commandments.

LEVI ISAAC OF BERDICHEV

A MAN SHOULD not rely on God to such an extent as to say, 'The Holy One, blessed be He, will deliver me, or He will do such-and-such for me.' But let him place his strength in the Holy One, blessed be He, trusting that He will help him if he strives to fulfil the commandments of the Torah and walk in the way of truth.

Zohar

A PERSON MUST not pray for his own concerns; rather he is to pray that the *Shekhinah* [Divine Presence] be redeemed from exile … even if one performs a *mitzvah* [commandment] but does not direct it for the sake of God, that is, he acts for some ulterior motive, he thereby brings about estrangement … For, as taught in the *Zohar*, the Torah and God are one, and if an individual performs a *mitzvah* properly, this *mitzvah* becomes one with God, one holy essence, constituted of one spiritual reality. On the other hand, if one performs it improperly he fashions an obstructing shell around the *mitzvah* so that it cannot unite itself with the holy essence of God.

SHLOMO OF LUTSK

HUMILITY

WHEN A person reaches the attribute of Nothingness, he realizes that he himself is nothing since God grants him existence.

LEVI ISAAC OF BERDICHEV

IT IS forbidden to accustom oneself to flattering speech.

Sefer Hasidim

HE SHOULD think of what will eventually take place and ponder his end.

KALONYMUS KALMAN EPSTEIN

HE MUST see himself as a worm, and look upon all other little creatures as companions in the world.

BAAL SHEM TOV

A PERSON should regard himself as nothing.

DOV BAER OF MEZHIRICH

T HE ROOT of humility is that man keeps himself far from the honour paid to noblemen.

ELEAZAR BEN JUDAH OF WORMS

C ARRY OUT all your good deeds in secret and walk humbly with thy God.

ELEAZAR BEN JUDAH OF WORMS

I T IS exceedingly difficult to possess the trait of humility since man's evil inclination entices him, so that he imagines himself to be one who has reached a high spiritual rank and in his own mind he becomes exalted and magnified. Consequently much effort is required in order to cast out the evil inclination and this notion from his heart.

KALONYMUS KALMAN EPSTEIN

NEVER BE proud.

JOSEPH CARO

ONCE A man attains to humility he becomes automatically stripped of his corporeality to some extent since haughtiness and pride stem from the corporeality and desires of this world.

KALONYMUS KALMAN EPSTEIN

IN PROPORTION to the extent that man succeeds in humbling himself, the more does he become stripped of his corporeality and the more does he remain in his purely spiritual state, so that he then attaches himself to the worlds on high.

KALONYMUS KALMAN EPSTEIN

THE HOLY One, blessed be He, magnifies only those who belittle themselves, and belittles only those who magnify themselves.

Zohar

WHOEVER IS small will be great; whoever is great will be small.

Zohar

HAPPY IS the man who belittles himself in this world. How great and exalted he will be in the next!

Zohar

A PERSON IS always in need of penance.

NAHMAN OF BRATSLAV

CHARITY

THE SECOND method involves giving charity properly on that day – this means that he should not know to whom he is giving, and the recipient should not have any knowledge of from whom he is receiving.

HAYYIM VITAL

GIVE CHARITY daily.

MORDECAI OF CHERNOBYL

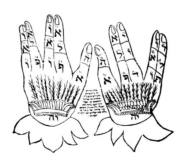

JOY

THE GREAT principle to pursue is equanimity.

BAAL SHEM TOV

HE IS to be joyful even in times of affliction.

HAYYIM VITAL

THE PRIMARY value of weeping comes when it is inspired by joy. Even the remorse for misdeed we experience is also of great value when it is inspired by joy.

NAHMAN OF BRATSLAV

THE SOUL is filled with love, bound with the bonds of love in great joy. This joy chases away all bodily pleasure and worldly delight from his heart. The powerful joy of love seizes his heart so that he continually thinks, 'How can I do God's will?' The pleasures of his children and the company of his wife are as nothing in comparison with the love of God.

ELEAZAR BEN JUDAH OF WORMS

WHEN RECITING the words, 'Give unto the Lord, O ye children of the mighty', a man should allow intense joy to enter his heart at the thought that we are called the children of the mighty, the children of Abraham, Isaac and Jacob.

ALEXANDER SUSSKIND

WHEN A person prays, studies Torah, or observes a commandment, he must be happy and joyful. He must have more pleasure than if he had reaped a great profit or had found a thousand gold coins.

HAYYIM VITAL

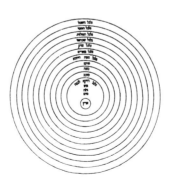

HYPOCRISY

ONE MUST not pressure another to eat when he knows that he will not eat, nor may one push presents to another when he knows he will not accept them.

Sefer Hasidim

SINCERITY OF heart means to serve God with the purest motives.

MOSES HAYYIM LUZZATTO

IT IS forbidden to accustom oneself to flattery. One must beware of saying what one does not mean; instead one must speak what is in his heart – one must match his speech with what he believes.

Sefer Hasidim

SIN

IF HE should find himself tempted to commit any transgression, let him recite the verses which caution against this transgression.

BAAL SHEM TOV

WHOEVER OPPRESSES people or terrorizes people will be treated in the next world like an animal.

Sefer Hasidim

EVEN IF a person, on confronting himself, should find that there is nothing good in him, that he is full of sin, and the evil impulse conspires to defeat him as a result of this by inducing in him depression and melancholy, he must not allow himself to be defeated by this.

NAHMAN OF BRATSLAV

WHY IS it that there is a righteous person who enjoys good, and there is a righteous person who suffers affliction? It is because in the latter case that righteous person was formerly wicked, and he is now suffering punishment. But is one punished for offences committed during one's youth? Did not Rabbi Simon say that the heavenly tribunal inflicts punishment only for evil conduct that takes place after a person is twenty?

He replied, 'I do not refer to misdeeds in the course of a person's life. I refer to the fact that a person pre-existed prior to his present life.'

Bahir

THE REMORSE felt by a person because of any wrongdoing he may have committed is veritably the pangs of hell meted out for that transgression.

ZADOK HAKOHEN OF LUBLIN

'PUT NOT your hand with the wicked' (Exod. 23:1); 'You shall not rob' (Lev. 19:13). These are the negative precepts. The postive precepts are: 'You shall surely open your hand' (Deut. 15:8); 'And you shall bind them for a sign upon your hand' (Deut. 6:8).

Eleazar ben Judah of Worms

'YOU SHALL not go up and down as a talebearer' (Lev. 19:16); 'And go not after other gods' (Jer. 25:6); 'And he that hastens with his feet sins' (Prov. 19:2). These are the negative precepts. The positive precepts are: 'After the Lord your God you shall walk' (Deut. 13:5); 'You shall walk in all the ways which the Lord your God has commanded you' (Deut. 5:33); 'Guard your foot when you go to the house of God' (Eccl. 5:1).

ELEAZAR BEN JUDAH OF WORMS

'YOU SHALL not commit adultery' (Exod. 20:13). This is the negative precept. The positive precepts are: 'And you, be fruitful and multiply' (Gen. 9:7), and circumcision.

ELEAZAR BEN JUDAH OF WORMS

HAVE YOUR sins always in mind and be anxious because of them.

JOSEPH CARO

WE ARE commanded to reprove the sinner in order to show the great love that we bear him, so that he might be spared punishment.

Zohar

H E IS to consider himself as a poor person and always speak gently and imploringly, as one who is poor.

BAAL SHEM TOV

T HE *TALMUD* states that the only real poverty is a poverty of enlightenment.

NAHMAN OF BRATSLAV

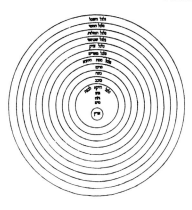

TORAH

THE TORAH is like a mirror in which a person only sees himself as he is.

MENAHEM MENDEL OF CHERNOBYL

I HEARD another reason why a penitent is better than a wholly righteous person. It is because he has experienced the passion of sin and when he repents and pursues the study of Torah and keeps the commandments, he does everything with great enthusiasm and desire since he knows the nature of enthusiasm. The wholly righteous person never experienced this.

DOV BAER OF MEZHIRICH

IF A MAN wishes to attain to the stage of refined prayer, with a stripping away of corporeality, great effort is required of him. He must study the Torah, carry out good deeds, and offer many supplications that he be worthy of attaining to pure prayer.

KALONYMUS KALMAN EPSTEIN

THE ROOT of the Torah is to study with profundity so as to know how to carry out God's commands.

ELEAZAR BEN JUDAH OF WORMS

STRIVE DAY and night to meditate on the Torah of the Lord.

ABRAHAM ABULAFIA

TAKE CARE never to allow your thoughts to dwell on anything other than the *Mishnah*, the Torah and the precepts. If any other thought enters your heart, cast it away.

JOSEPH CARO

WISDOM

GOD GRACED man with the capacity of speech and with fullness of perception and comprehension, but the greatest gift He bestowed on him is wisdom.

BAHYA IBN PAKUDA

THE DESIRABLE pursuits of this world, though they are of a physical nature, are desirable in the eyes of God and they lead a person to eternal life.

JUDAH LOEW OF PRAGUE

WISDOM IS the food of the soul.

ABRAHAM ABULAFIA

GAZE WITH divine intelligence into the works of the kabbalists. Here you will discover that which you seek and you will see that they all cry out in protest against the absence of wisdom.

ABRAHAM ABULAFIA

THE CATEGORY of a wise man refers to one who absorbs himself in the contemplation of wisdom to a point of self-effacement.

MENAHEM MENDEL OF VITEBSK

GIVE TO the wise and he will become even wiser.

BAAL SHEM TOV

WISDOM ACTUALLY derives benefit from folly, because if stupidity did not exist, wisdom's worth would go unrecognized.

Zohar

ALL THE divisions of wisdom, according to their respective subject matter, are gates the Creator, praised be He, opened to rational beings through which to understand the Torah and the world.

BAHYA IBN PAKUDA

THE TRAIT of sadness is a very bad quality, especially for one who wishes to attain wisdom.

HAYYIM VITAL

GLOSSARY

Aggadah
    rabbinic scriptural
    commentary
Asiyah
    making
Ayin
    nothing
Ayn Sof
    infinite
Bahir
    Book of Light
Beriyah
    creation
Binah
    understanding
Devekut
    cleaving to God
Elohim
    God
Gemara
    Talmud
Gematriot
    mystical calculation
Hasidei Ashkenaz
    the pious of Germany
Hasiduth
    pietism
Hayyot
    living creatures
Hekhalot
    Heavenly halls

Hokhmah
    Wisdom
Kabbalah
    Jewish mysticism
Merkavah
    Divine chariot
Mikvah
    ritual bath
Mishnah
    second-century rabbinic code of law
Mitzvah
    commandment
Rebbe
    spiritual leader
Sefer Yetsirah
    Book of Creation
Sefirot
    Divine emanations
Shekhinah
    Divine presence
Sitra Ahra
    the other side
Talmud
    sixth-century rabbinic code of law
Tikkun
    cosmic repair
Zaddik
    holy person
Zohar
    illumination

CHRONOLOGICAL TABLE

Patriarchal period
  c. 1900–c. 1600 BCE
Exodus
  c. 1250–c. 1230 BCE
Period of the Judges
  c. 1200–c. 1000 BCE
Period of the United Monarchy
  c. 1030–c. 930 BCE
Division of the Kingdoms
  c. 930 BCE
Destruction of the Northern
  Kingdom (Israel) by the
  Assyrians
  722 BCE
Destruction of the Southern
  Kingdom (Judah) by the
  Babylonians
  586 BCE
Babylonian Exile
  586–538 BCE
Return of the Exiles
  538 BCE
Rebuilding of the Temple
  c. 529–c. 515 BCE
Second Temple period
  c. 515 BCE–c.70 CE
End of the period of prophecy
  c. 450 BCE
Hellenistic period
  333–63 BCE

Maccabean rebellion and
  Hasmonean period
  167–163 BCE
Hasmonean revolt
  166–164 BCE
Roman period
  c. 146 BCE–c. 400 CE
Philo of Alexandria
first century BCE
New Testament written
  c. 50–90
Jewish rebellion against Rome
  66–70
Siege and destruction of Jerusalem
  and the Second Temple
  70
Mishnaic period
  c. 100–c. 200 CE
Bar Kokhba revolt
  c. 150
Mishnah compiled
  c. 200
Sefer Yetsirah
  second century
Talmudic period
  c. 200–c. 600
Jerusalem *Talmud* compiled
  c. fifth century
Medieval period
  c. 600–c. 1600

Hekhalot literature
c. 200–c. 1300

Geonic period
c. 600–c. 1300

Hai Gaon
939–1038

Bahya Ibn Pakuda
eleventh century

Hananel ben Hushiel
eleventh century

Crusades
1095–1291

Moses Maimonides
1135–1204

Bahir
c. twelfth century

Jacob of Marvège
twelfth–thirteenth century

Hasidei Ashkenaz
twelfth–thirteenth century

Eleazar ben Judah of Worms
c. 1165–c. 1230

Azriel of Gerona
early thirteenth century

Abraham Abulafia
1240–after 1292

Joseph Gikatilla
1248–c. 1325

Isaac of Acco
thirteenth–fourteenth century

Zohar
c. thirteenth century

Abraham ben Isaac of Granada
c. fourteenth century

Joseph Tzayach
1505–73

Joseph Caro
1488–1575

Moses Cordovero
1522–70

Judah Loew of Prague
1525–1609

Isaac Luria
1534–72

Jacob Zemah
d. after 1665

Hayyim Vital
1543–1620

Shabbetai Zevi
1626–76

Zechariah Mendel of Jaroslaw
seventeenth century

Modern period
c. 1700–present

Moses Hayyim Luzzatto
1707–46

Baal Shem Tov (Besht)
1700–60

Mystics of Bet El
c. eighteenth century

Elimelech of Lyzhansk
1717–87

Vilna Gaon
1720–97

Menahem Mendel of Chernobyl
    1730–89
Menahem Mendel of Vitebsk
    1730–88
Hayyim of Volozhin
    1749–1821
Shlomo of Lutsk
    eighteenth century
Alexander Susskind
    eighteenth century
Hayyim Haykl of Amdur
    eighteenth century
Nahman of Bratslav
    1772–1811
Levi Isaac of Berdichev
    c. 1740–1810
Jacob Joseph of Polonnoye
    eighteenth century
Kalonymus Kalman Epstein
    nineteenth century

Dov Baer of Mezhirich
    c. 1710–72
Shneur Zalman of Liady
    1747–1813
Mordecai of Chernobyl
    1770–1837
Dov Baer of Lubavich
    nineteenth century
Isaac Judah Jahiel Safrin
    1806–74
Zadok HaKohen of Lublin
    1823–1900
Abraham Isaac Kook
    1865–1935
Aaron Roth
    1894–1944
The Holocaust
    1942–5
State of Israel
    1948

ACKNOWLEDGEMENTS

The publisher would like to thank Sonia Halliday Photographs for assistance and permission to produce the following pictures:

Pages viii, 41, 120, a barmitzvah holding a Yad while reading from the Torah; pages xii, 45, sunset near Hebron; pages xvii, 48, 125, aerial view of the River Jordan and the Sea of Galilee; pages xxi, 100, 128, engraving by J. Salmon, 1840, depicting the Synagogue of the Jews in Jerusalem; pages 25, 104, 133, the Sinai Mountains, Israel, at dawn; pages 29, 108, 136, Moses and the tablets and the golden calf, from Great Witley Church; pages 33, 113, 141, the River Jordan south of Galilee at sunrise; pages 37, 117, 144, Elijah in the chariot of fire, from the Winchester Bible.